Get Hooked

Learn to Crochet with **Tom Daley**

Get Hooked

Learn to Crochet with **Tom Daley**

15 easy to follow **crochet patterns** for your wardrobe and home

Including patterns that first appeared in *Made With Love*

PHOTOGRAPHY BY DANIEL FRASER

Contents

06 Introduction

16 How to Use This Book

20 Yarn Essentials

30 Crochet Essentials

76 Crochet Accessories

- 78 Kit Bag
- 84 Friendship Bracelets
- 88 Tote Bag
- 94 Bottle Carrier
- 98 Bucket Hat
- 102 Cosy Slippers
- 112 Heart Keyring

112 Crochet Garments

- 114 Polo Shirt
- 122 Motif Vest
- 128 Random Stripe Sweater

TOM DALEY

134
Crochet Homewares

136 Plant Pots
140 Shaggy Cushion
144 Alphabet Bunting
152 Chevron Throw
156 Granny Square Cushion

162
Caring For Your Makes

170
How to...

171 Gift Your Makes
172 Fit Crochet into Your Day
175 Manage Your Yarn Stash
176 Be Mindful as You Make
178 Crochet With Upcycled Yarns
179 Prolong the Life of Your Garment
181 Own Your Making

184 Recommended Yarns
186 Thank Yous
188 Index

GET HOOKED

Introduction →

As an athlete, my diving training and competing schedules mean that I travel a lot. Whenever I'm packing for those long periods away from home, the very first things that I put in my bag are my crochet hooks and yarn (alongside my diving trunks, of course). Nowadays they go everywhere with me. I crochet on planes, I crochet on trains, I crochet in hotel beds, I even crochet poolside. I love how portable it is as a craft, which means that I can pick up my hook and work a few stitches when I have some downtime or if I'm feeling anxious at a competition and need a distraction during the stressful waits between dives.

I took up knitting first, which I loved and still love, but swiftly moved on to crochet too. I just adore the variety of stitches and effects that can be achieved with only a crochet hook and a length of yarn. If you can imagine it, then you can crochet it! I've made everything from a stuffed unicorn toy for a baby to a Gucci-inspired dress for my friend Sophie and, of course, a pair of stripey trunks for me. In fact, the trunks were the first crochet project I made to my own design, without following a pattern. I based them on an pair of trunks that I already owned, tweaking the shape to make them fit. Since then, I haven't looked back.

Crochet has become an important outlet for my creativity. I'm not afraid of wearing a splash of colour, so being able to crochet my own garments means I'm not restricted to what's available in stores. Because high-street stores are trying to appeal to the widest number of people, they more often than not play it safe with black, grey and navy, whereas I want to wear the rainbow. We should all be able to wear whatever makes us feel good and allows us to shine.

Another brilliant thing about crochet is how quickly the fabric can grow. Depending on the stitch pattern, the negative spaces (or holes) between the different stitches can be just as important as the stitch itself in creating the desired effect; that's why crochet can be incredibly quick to do. The very first thing I ever crocheted was a bobble hat for Robbie, which I made just as I was about to head off on a training camp. I wanted to make something that he could wear while I was away so that we could feel close to each other. In less than an hour, I'd made a cute hat that he loved wearing as much as I loved making it – we both knew that I had poured love into every stitch.

As well as immense joy, crochet brings an important sense of calm to my life. It's a form meditation that allows me to take my mind off other things. Initially, knitting and crochet were ways to escape from the stress of competing at diving events, during those long waits between dives. Now, no matter where I am, I can get lost in the stitches and exist completely in the moment – everything else melts away.

In crochet, I've found a creative outlet that allows me to express my true self, which gives me so much joy. I've also found a supportive online band of fellow crocheters who all generously share their knowledge and talents. When I first started to share what I was making on Instagram, I was blown away by all the lovely comments – they really gave me the confidence to keep making and experimenting. I've benefitted from the love, support and encouragement of others all the way along my crocheting journey, and now I want to pass that on. I hope that, in turn, I can inspire you to try this amazing craft and get hooked!

How I started

Crochet was the natural next step for me after I took up knitting in 2020. I'd only been knitting for around six months when I made my first attempts at crochet and it's no exaggeration to say that I was instantly hooked. It was during the COVID-19 pandemic – those long months when it was necessary for us all to stay at home – that I first picked up a crochet hook to while away those hours when I couldn't train in the gym or practise at the pool. Crochet gave me something productive to do during those lockdowns, which I found really rewarding. It made me put down my phone and pick up some yarn instead, but it also kept my mind occupied as well as my hands. Crochet now gives me something to do when competing that also challenges my brain, so that I'm not only focussing on the competition in between dives.

For me, the unique position we all found ourselves in during lockdown led to this new life of crafting, one that I had never even considered before. It soon became an all-consuming passion. Maybe it's because of my competitive streak as a sportsperson, but I very quickly became very committed to crochet and practised whenever I could. I had a bit of a head start when it came to crochet, as knitting had got me used to working with needles and handling yarn, but it still took lots of practice attempts before I got comfortable with using the hook and maintaining an even tension on the yarn.

I'm now so comfortable with crochet that I will do it whenever I get the chance. I have even crocheted on TV. When I took part in *The Great British Bake Off* for the Stand Up to Cancer charity fundraiser, I crocheted with edible strawberry laces to make the decorations that sat on top of my showstopper cake. Now that's not something I ever thought I would be doing when I first picked up a crochet hook! The theme for the showstopper was 'my perfect day off', so of course I chose to bake a knitting and crochet-themed layer cake.

When I first began to crochet and knit, people couldn't quite believe that I had made the garments and accessories that I was wearing myself, so I continued to share what I was making online, posting my progress on Instagram. It was only when I was photographed knitting at the Tokyo Olympics during the summer of 2021, sat up in the supporters stand, that lots of people started to show an interest. Nowadays millions of people watch me crochet online, which I find mind blowing. If I can inspire just one of those people to learn to crochet and enjoy the same benefits that I get from it, then that will make me very happy indeed!

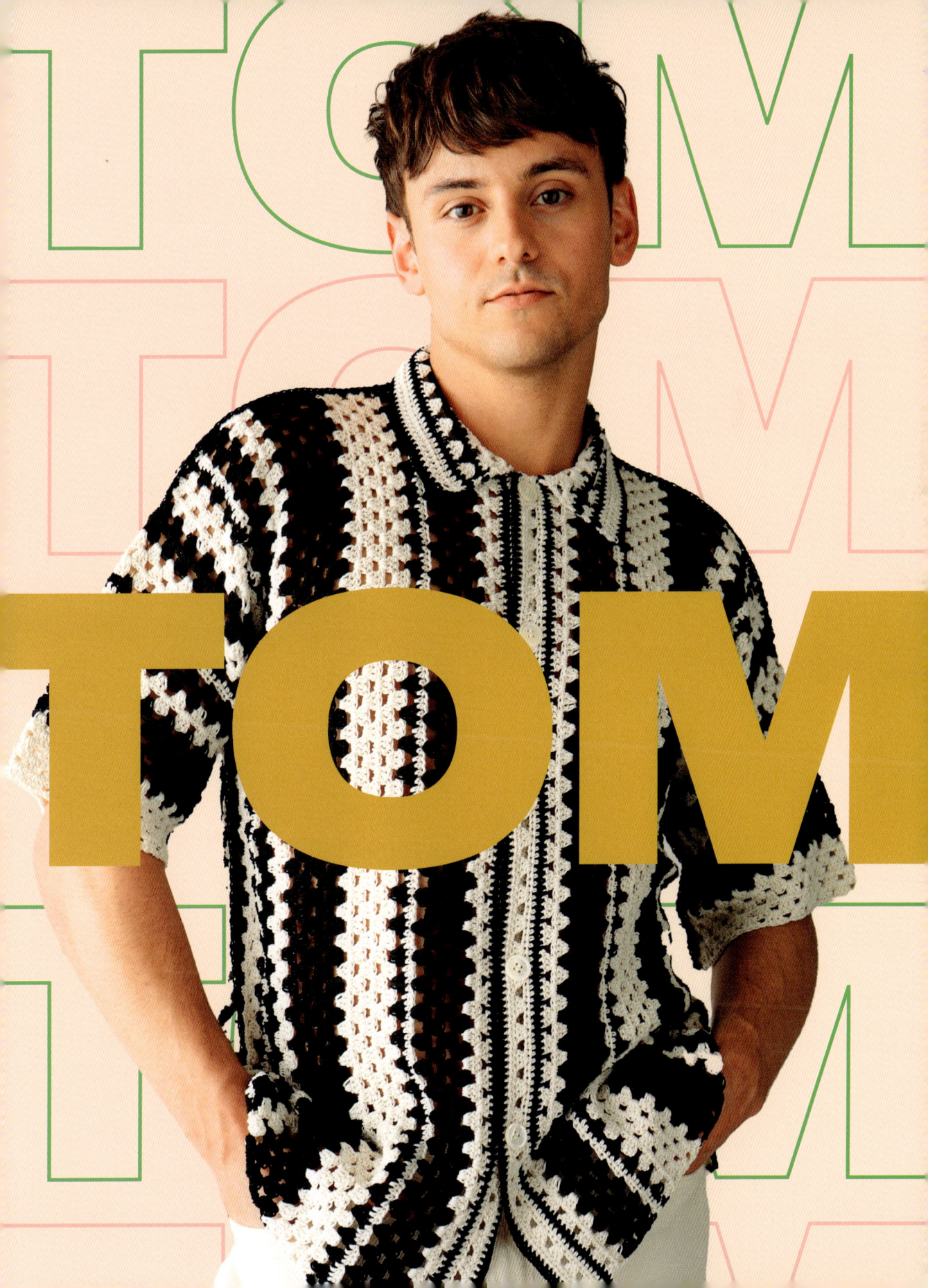

"**Crochet is my** *happy* **place.**"

TOM DALEY

Meditate through making

Despite both being slow crafts, all the crocheters and knitters I know have loads of energy and find it really hard to sit still. I include myself in that description. I find crochet to be an easy way of shutting out the rest of the world – it allows me to focus on the task in hand, empty my mind of extraneous thoughts and simply relax. Plus it's a really productive thing to do in my free time, rather than doom-scrolling on my phone. When I was at my most active and didn't know how to slow down, or recovering from an injury and forced to stop, crochet allowed me to pause and put my feet up.

For many years I have meditated every day using apps like Headspace, but crochet has given me a new space to be meditative and now I choose crochet over other forms of meditation. Though people have been knitting and crocheting for centuries, it's only recently that these crafts have been recognised by scientists for their therapeutic qualities. They've now been proven to have a host of physical and mental well-being benefits. Research has shown crochet and knitting can help with anxiety and depression, reduce stress and distract from chronic pain, as well as reduce loneliness and isolation.

For me, I find crocheting a way to re-set, in the same way as meditating or using breathing techniques. It takes me away from everything else and completely quietens my mind because I have to focus on exactly what I'm doing – both the pattern instructions and the repetitive movement – so there's no space for other thoughts. It's the perfect level of concentration and because it's so repetitive, it's very calming. If I'm having a bad day, I can do ten minutes of crochet and re-start with a clearer and more positive outlook. I even sometimes use it as a tool between work tasks, so I start each one fresh. Crochet is ideal for those moments when you may otherwise mindlessly reach for your phone to scroll through your social media feed or head to the cupboard for a snack because you are bored. It facilitates a moment of peacefulness and productivity. I used to be a terrible nail-biter but since I started knitting and crocheting, I have stopped gnawing at my nails.

Whilst some projects can take a long time to complete, and become UFOs (that's Un-Finished-Objects) in your project basket, the slow-moving and gentle nature of yarn crafts is all part of the enjoyment. Okay, you can't crochet a sweater in a day but when you do finish – whether that's many days, weeks or even months later – it just feels more rewarding. This is the whole beauty of it. Don't put any time pressure on yourself, just be present in the process.

I also love to take my crochet outdoors and it's the perfect portable craft for travelling too. During the Tokyo Olympics in 2021, I would sit outside on my hotel balcony, when the sun was setting over the horizon, and crochet. I find that being outdoors in nature adds another level of calm, so pick up your yarn and hook and head out to your backyard, garden or a local park to crochet and see how you feel. But be prepared to be approached by fellow crocheters, who may not be able to resist taking a closer look and commenting on your work, or sharing their own stories.

One of the most wonderful things about crochet is that it can be really sociable activity, as well as a solitary one. A craft club can be a great way to meet like-minded practitioners, share stories, swap tips and improve your skills. Find a nearby group through your local yarn store, via Facebook or Ravelry, or why not set up your own crochet circle with friends.

Love

Made with...

Made with love for those you love

There's something truly special about making something by hand for a friend, loved one or new baby, or even a new puppy. With a handmade gift, you know that the person who made it has really taken time and care and been invested in each tiny stitch. Although it's very easy to go online and buy a gift with the single click of a button for next day delivery, creating a handmade gift takes time and effort that cannot be exchanged or imitated, and which the recipient will find all the more precious. Plus it will be the only gift like it on the entire planet, so it does not get more personal than that!

I love the fact that I can create something unique for someone, tailor-made to suit their style and tastes and completely personalised to them. All of the projects in this book are designed to be recipes that you can adapt and customise to suit you or the person you are making it for; that's the beauty of making something by hand rather than buying "off the shelf". One of the first items I made was a scarf for my mum for Mother's Day and I was able to choose a purple yarn, which is her favourite colour. I have always found seeing the reactions of my friends and family when I gift them something that I have made really special and that's all part of the fun for me.

In *Get Hooked*, I have included the patterns for some of my favourite items for gifting. From a pair of cosy slippers for toes both large and small to a crocheted plant holder to carry a housewarming pot plant, I hope these thoughtful gifts will surprise and delight the recipient.

How I approach design

I love the process of choosing yarns, colours, stitch textures and shapes when making items for my favourite people. From picking out the softest and warmest fibres, to deciding on acid brights or soft pastel colours, it's so individual. I draw inspiration from so many places; from watching reels on Instagram to flicking through editorial fashion shoots in magazines, from couture collections on the runway to the street style I see every day outside my front door in London.

I love using vivid colours for my makes. Sometimes I find that when you're buying ready-to-wear from a store, the rationale is to buy black or grey or another muted colour that goes with everything. Or you're limited to those colours that the fashion brands have decided that everyone must wear that season. But if you're choosing to make something from scratch, you have the choice to put any colours you like into it. Plus with crochet, you can choose the fibre from which the fabric will be made too!

For each project in this book, I have given the yarn and shade that I have used, but you can make it any colour or yarn you want – just make sure to work a tension swatch (see page 74) before you dive into the project if you are substituting the yarn. I have included some of my favourite contemporary pastels and popping neons alongside classic and dramatic monochromes. But if you want to substitute the colour for all black or bright pink and lime green? Go for it! Show your personality through what you make.

Once you have an understanding of how the different knitting stitches and techniques work and how to use them to create fabrics and shapes, you can get creative and experiment. One of the greatest things about crochet is that it really doesn't matter too much if something goes wrong. I have made many things in the past, where the sleeves didn't quite fit or the sizing came up a bit off. I even once made a sweater that I couldn't get over my head! If this happens, don't panic. You can simply unravel your work and start again. It's just another opportunity to practise your craft and improve your skills. My advice is always just to enjoy the process, even if it doesn't go perfectly every time – it's all part of the crochet journey!

How to Use This Book

Whether you have yet to pick up a
crochet hook for the first time or
you are a seasoned pro who crochets
away, I hope this book will inspire
you to take some time for yourself
and to start a new project. I have
worked with some of my favourite yarns
and colours to make fun, original and
vibrant creations — I hope you love
them as much as I do!

In this section, I guide you through all the basics, from making a foundation row or ring to working the core crochet stitches through to fastening off and making up a project. Then I share my favourite designs for creating quick-to-make accessories and simple homewares up to more complex garments, some with stitch textures, some with colourwork and some with both!

I also demystify the cryptic code of crochet, which can sometimes read like a foreign language! Once you get started and become familiar with a few key terms, it's not as complex as it looks – I promise! I do think it's a bit like learning an unfamiliar language or taking up a new sport – it just takes a bit of practice to become proficient.

Have you ever heard of the concept of muscle memory? The more you repeat a movement, the easier you find it and soon it becomes second nature. Before long, you'll be able to crochet while chatting or watching a boxset. Give it a week or two and you'll be hooked (pun intended)!

The speed at which you decide to work through the projects in this book is entirely up to you. If you're a more experienced crocheter, you may wish to dip in and out of the designs that call loudest to you, but if you're a beginner, start by checking the skill level assigned to each project.

Take as long as you need to hone each new skill and refer back to the 'how to' guides; while crocheted fabric can be quick to grow, the beauty of crochet is that it's a slow craft – a moment to unwind and get lost in your making – and that's all part of the enjoyment. If you drop a stitch or make a hole, don't stress! It's never a disaster. You can always unravel a few rounds or rows and re-work them.

Got pressing things to do that are not crochet-related? Although it will become hard to imagine what could be more important – don't worry about that either. You can always put your hook down once you've worked a few stitches and then pick it up again whenever you have a spare moment. Just be sure to keep your WIP (work in progress) safely away from pets, children and nosy housemates. Most of all, just enjoy the process and the endless possibilities of what you can create.

Happy hooking!

HOW TO USE THIS BOOK

Sizing

All the garments in this book are designed to be unisex and inclusive for all. Many people think that unisex items lean more towards boxy men's shapes that women can also wear. I like to think of it almost in reverse – flattering shapes that anyone can wear. Ultimately, you should always wear whatever makes you feel good.

Choosing a garment size

Sometimes it can be tricky to know the right garment size to crochet from a pattern. Don't just plump for your usual clothing size as that may not match the dimensions that the pattern designer has used – every garment is designed to have a certain amount of ease, which differs from project to project. Ordinarily, garments are listed in generic sizes, such as small, medium, large and so on, but they will also include key measurements, such as the chest measurement. Children's garments are more usually presented as an age range, from 4 to 5 years, for example.

If you're unsure what size to choose, my advice is this: for comparison, take the measurements of your favourite sweater, cardigan or other garment that is similar in shape and fabric weight to the one you plan to make. This garment can be as tight-fitting or as loose-fitting as you wish, but bear in mind the amount of ease that has been designed into the garment you plan to make. Lie your existing garment flat and measure the chest width. Now find the closest match to that width on the size chart – that's the best size for you and the one that you're going to highlight to follow.

Following the pattern instructions

Pattern instructions will be written in more than one size. The smallest will be first and sit just outside the parentheses and then the larger sizes will follow inside the parentheses. When there is only one figure given in the instructions, this will apply to all sizes. When there is a 0 listed, then no stitches or rows are worked for that specific size. Remember this: if your size is the second in the size chart, it will always be the second in any sequence.

To ensure you always work the correct size when following lengthy pattern instructions, I advise highlighting or underlining the figures that correspond with your size in the pattern. This includes the number of balls of yarn you'll need to complete your project, the number of stitches to be made in the foundation row or round, the number of stitches or rows worked in a certain stitch pattern or colour, the number of times to repeat an instruction or the length of any section in centimetres or inches. Marking your specific size within the instructions simplifies reading the pattern as you work – your eyes can flick straight to the correct number. If your pattern is in a book like this one, you may prefer to photocopy the relevant page.

Checking your tension

Before you start any new project, always check your tension or gauge (see page 66). If your tension varies from that given in the pattern by even one stitch or row, change your crochet hook size up or down accordingly otherwise your garment will end up a different size from the dimensions stated on the size chart. Over a larger piece, any difference in tension or gauge will be further exaggerated.

Yarn Essentials

There are many different types of yarns available in a multitude of fibres, colours, and textures. Yarn is one of my favourite things; I even got a yarn advent calendar one year for Christmas! When selecting the yarn for any project, the two most important factors are fibre and weight.

A quick guide

Fibre

Anything can be used as a yarn – as long as it is a continuous length that can be crocheted, it can be done. Yarns are broadly split into different categories.

1 • Animal fibres

Sheep's wool, alpaca, mohair, and silk are all examples of animal fibres. Wool is a firm favourite with crocheters. Spun from the fleece of a sheep, it's durable and a great insulator so will keep you at the right temperature. It can also absorb moisture without feeling wet. Great for bobble hats in rainy weather! It can feel a bit scratchy against the skin, but different sheep breeds produce wool with various qualities. Merino wool is spun from the fleece of that breed of sheep and is softer than regular wool.

2 • Plant fibres

Cotton, hemp, bamboo, and linen are examples of plant fibres. These are non-allergenic and cooling, so are ideal for warmer months. Cotton is one of my go-to yarns for summer knits.

3 • Synthetic fibres

Nylon, acrylic, and polyester are all synthetic fibres. These tend to be inexpensive, wash well, and are easy to care for. These yarns are particularly hard-wearing so are ideal for items that you might use every day like cushions and throws. Synthetics are sometimes blended with natural fibres to enhance washability and strength. The synthetic fibres can help bind yarns like wool together to stop shedding or shrinking.

Whilst synthetic yarns may not seem as appealing as animal or natural fibres, they are becoming the favourite choice of vegans. If you're looking for yarns made from non-animal fibre sources or are concerned about the consumption of water or other natural resources in the production of some yarns, there is an increasing number of synthetic options available.

Weight

All these fibres are spun to create yarns that are made up of one or more plies – or strands – twisted together. Some yarns are more twisted than others so have a slightly different quality, but generally it gives a yarn strength, making it harder to break when working with it.

Two single strands twisted together make a 2-ply yarn, or if eight are used, this is an 8-ply. The thickness of the yarn is decided by the thickness of the individual plies, not the number of plies, so a 4-ply yarn is not necessarily thicker than a single ply, but the general rule is the lower the number of plies, the finer the yarn. I love bulky roving yarns – which are long and narrow fibres – as the projects work up so quickly. I just love the personality of these yarns!

While I prefer crocheting with bulky yarns as your work grows so quickly, such a heavyweight yarn isn't suitable for every project. Each yarn is classified as a certain weight, which refers to the thickness of the overall yarn. They can be lace weight or superfine through to super bulky or jumbo. As a general rule, the weights of yarns fall within standardised categories assigned by the Craft Yarn Council in the U.S. to help knitters and crocheters choose the right thickness of yarn to ensure every project is a success (see page 24).

Yarn weight category and symbol	LACE	SUPER FINE	FINE	LIGHT	MEDIUM	BULKY	SUPER BULKY	JUMBO
Type of yarns in category	2-ply (fingering)	3-ply (sock), baby	4-ply (sport), baby	Double knitting (light worsted)	Aran (worsted), afghan	Chunky (bulky), craft, rug	Super chunky (super bulky)	Jumbo
Crochet tension (gauge) in double (single) crochet to 10cm (4 inches)	32–42 sts	21–32 sts	16–20 sts	12–17 sts	11–14 sts	8–11 sts	7–9 sts	6 sts and fewer
Recommended crochet hook in metric size	Steel hook 1.6–1.4mm	2.25–3.5mm	3.5–4.5mm	4.5–5.5mm	5.5–6.5mm	6.5–9mm	9–15mm	15mm and larger
Recommended crochet hook in U.S. size	Steel hook 6, 7, 8	B-1 to E-4	E-4 to 7	7 to 1-9	1-9 to K-10½	K-10½ to M-13	M-13 to Q	Q and larger
Knit tension (gauge) in stocking (stockinette) stitch to 10cm (4 inches)	33–40 sts	27–32 sts	23–26 sts	21–24 sts	16–20 sts	12–15 sts	7–11 sts	6 sts and fewer
Recommended knitting needles in metric size	1.5–2.25mm	2.25–3.25mm	3.25–3.75mm	3.75–4.5mm	4.5–5.5mm	5.5–8mm	8–12.75mm	12.75mm and larger
Recommended knitting needles in U.S. size	000–1	1–3	3–5	5–7	7–9	9–11	11–17	17 and larger

Worsted is a medium-weight yarn and sits in the middle of the range. It's often used for hats, scarves, sweaters, and a myriad of other items because you can see the individual stitches. For beginners, I always suggest starting with a chunkier yarn, so bulky is my go-to choice. Once you have got to grips with the most comfortable way to hold the yarn and let it flow, your crochet will grow quite fast and that feels really rewarding.

Fibre choice is also important when starting out. Generally, I would recommend wool because it has a natural elasticity and is quite forgiving. A wool blend or super-wash wool is a good choice because as a blended synthetic fibre, it flows more easily. Cotton is also lovely to work with because it's strong and unlikely to break but is flat with less stretch and a bit slower to work with. I would go for something mid-range – a decent quality but not too expensive!

As part of the instructions for every project in this book, you will see the recommended weight of yarn to use. If you're shopping in store and don't know what you need – just ask. I would also consider the availability of what you need – the last thing you want to do is run out of yarn mid-project! In my opinion, it's best to buy a bit too much yarn so this doesn't happen and then use up any yarn remnants in smaller projects (see page 175 for my yarn stash-busting tips). Within the projects, there are a few smaller items that are ideal for smaller amounts of yarn.

Label talk

Yarn is packaged in different ways, but it will always be accompanied by a yarn label, which is sometimes called a ball band. The yarn is wound like a ball, skein, hank, or on a cone – basically in different shapes – with a helpful label, which you must always read carefully.

Shade names and dye lot numbers

Some brands label their yarns with a code for each different colour they offer. However, I prefer it when a yarn range has a name for each shade rather than a code number. Especially when the name is an evocative description of the shade of the yarn.

Crocheters sometimes talk about dye lots, but what exactly does this mean? Well, yarns are available in many different natural and dyed colours. A dye lot is a batch of yarn that has been dyed at the same time, so even if yarns have the same shade name or code number, if they're dyed at different times, this means the colour could vary because of differences in temperature, dyeing time, and other factors. When you're buying yarn, make sure all the balls or skeins have been dyed in the same lot (they will have the same unique number) so the colour of the yarn is consistent throughout your project.

TOM'S TIP:

If you're giving a crocheted item as a gift, include a yarn label (ball band) in the parcel so the recipient knows how to care for it and won't shrink it in the wash. If it's something for yourself or a family member, take a photo of the label so you can always refer back to the care instructions.

Reading yarn labels

Yarn labels are all slightly different and laid out in a variety of ways, but most packaging includes the following information:

The name of the brand.

The name of the yarn.

The **weight category** of the yarn (and if the yarn is from a U.S. manufacturer, also the relevant Craft Yarn Council symbol).

The **weight of the yarn** in grams or ounces that is packaged in the ball, skein, hank or cone.

The **length of the yarn** in metres and/or yards.

The **fibre content**, including the percentages of each type of fibre that makes up the yarn.

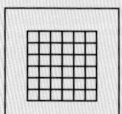

The colour information, including the **shade name or number** and the **dye lot number**.

The **recommended knitting needle or crochet hook size** to achieve the given tension (gauge).

The **recommended tension (gauge)**, including number of stitches and rows to 10cm (4 in) (see page 66).

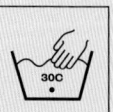

Care instructions, including washing, drying, and ironing – these instructions apply to the yarn as to any finished crocheted item.

Yarn Essentials

Buying yarn

Yarns are held together in various ways and packages for sale, and the general way they are presented is called "put-ups". This includes balls, hanks, and skeins in various weights.

Ball

A ball of yarn is usually wound roughly by hand into a spherical shape. The working end of the yarn is on the outside of the ball, which will move around a fair bit when in use.

Hank

A hank is an attractive, loosely wound coil of yarn that is then twisted into a rope. It's usually the more delicate yarns that are sold in hanks. Before working with the yarn, you need to untwist the hank and then wind the yarn into a ball by hand, or you can use a ball winder. As you wind the untwisted hank into a ball, check the yarn for any faults or knots.

Cone

These yarns are machine wound onto stiff cardboard or plastic cones. They can often be quite heavy as the cones can store large quantities of yarn.

Skein

In a skein, the yarn is wound into a loose, oblong or donut shape. Skeins are ready to use – just find the working end from inside the centre. A skein doesn't move around too much when in use.

Substituting yarn

Yarn substitution is a term that describes using a different yarn to the one recommended in the pattern. With so many yarns available, understanding how to substitute one yarn for another is so useful. It gives you lots more choice when thinking about your next project and sourcing supplies. There are several reasons why you may want to substitute a yarn - maybe you're looking for a vegan-friendly alternative to animal fibres, or a yarn that's more affordable, or the recommended yarn is no longer available. You may even spot a yarn that you love and want to make something with it. It took me a while to feel confident with subbing yarns, but here are my tips for things to think about:

1 • Check the tension

The first step is to always check the tension (gauge). You will need to crochet a decent-sized swatch before continuing with your project. As well as ensuring your swatch gives the right tension (gauge), the designer will have ensured that the stitch pattern works with the yarn to create a certain effect. Solid-coloured and smooth yarns will give greater stitch definition than multi-coloured or tweedy yarns, for example. Even if something is 5mm (¼ inch) out, it may have a real impact on the size of the shape of the garment or the finished item.

2 • Think about fibre

When subbing yarns, look for alternatives with a similar fibre content, so they have a tension (gauge) close to the recommended yarn. Any slight difference between yarns may have a big knock-on effect on the way the stitches look. Generally, plant-based fibres don't have as much stretch as animal fibres, unless they're blended with elastane, acrylic, or polyester. The same garment designed in stretchy wool will look quite different when made up in flat cotton. A common substitution is a wool yarn for a wool blend yarn.

3 • Calculate the meterage

It's important to check the meterage (yardage) – the length of the yarn within the ball, skein, or hank – compared to the one you're substituting. This is so you don't run out of yarn, midway through your project. Every pattern will tell you how much yarn you need, so divide the amount specified in the pattern by the meterage (yardage) of the balls you want, to know what number to buy.

4 • Weigh everything up

While it's a good idea to stick with the recommended yarn weight, you can experiment by substituting two strands of light weight yarn for a single strand in a heavier weight. Remember to calculate the amount of yarn in metres or yards needed to complete the project. Doubling up yarns to create an interesting colour or textural effect (see page 139) is not an exact science, so your tension (gauge) is the best guide.

Crochet Essentials

02-

If you're new to crochet, you only need just a few items to get you started. It really requires very little equipment, just a hook, some yarn and a pair of scissors for snipping your yarn. You can read more about yarns on pages 22-28.

Crochet kit list

Choosing the right crochet hook

Crochet hooks come in a variety of sizes and are also made in different materials, including metal, wood, and plastic. I started with a set of basic metal crochet hooks I found online. As I crocheted more and more, I started to experiment with other hooks to find out what works best for me.

Standard hook sizes span from 2mm to 10mm (US 4 to N/P-15). Most people have a favourite hook size to use. For me, this is a 4mm or 4.5mm (US G/6) hook, but it depends on the weight of the yarn you're using. Basically, the thicker the yarn, the chunkier the hook. The smallest hooks are specialist lace hooks and these range from 0.6mm to 1.75mm and are metal. The largest hooks are 10mm (US N/P-15) and are used for making bulkier crocheted items. Check the yarn label (ball band) on any yarn – it will be labelled with the recommended size of hook to work with (see page 26). One of the best things about crochet is how quickly it grows at first, even with a standard 4mm (US G/6) hook!

You want to make sure that whatever style of hook you use, it's comfortable to hold; you just have to figure out what you prefer. The handle of a crochet hook is most often straight with an indentation for the grip (see below). However, some hooks have ergonomically shaped handles with a thumb rest to make them comfortable to hold.

Nowadays, I try to make more sustainable choices with my crafting. My favourite crochet hooks to use are made from bamboo because, like bamboo knitting needles, they're warm to the touch and recyclable.

Hook size conversion chart

metric	2.00	2.25	2.50	2.75	3.25	3.50	3.75	4.00	5.00	5.50	6.00	6.50	8.00	9.00	10.00
imperial	14	13	12	11	10	9	8	7	6	5	4	3	0	00	000
U.S.	4	B-1	1/0	C-2	D-3	E-4	F-5	G-6	H-8	I-9	J-10	K10½	L-11	M/N-13	N/P-15

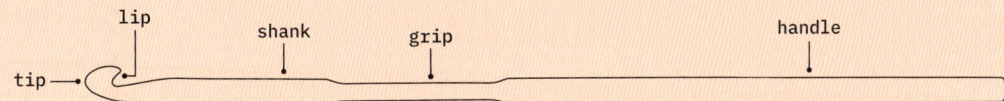

Crochet Essentials

Crochet basics →

With these instructions, you can go from a beginner to a fully-fledged crocheter in no time. If you're left-handed, simply hold the hook and yarn in the exact mirror image of the techniques shown here for right-handed crocheters.

Holding the crochet hook

Finding the most comfortable way to hold your crochet hook can just be a case of experimenting until you find the most natural position for you. There are two main ways to hold a crochet hook:

Like a knife

In your right hand, hold the hook with your hand over the hook and your palm facing down. Place your thumb on one side and your fingers on the other side. Grip the hook exactly like you would when holding a knife to cut food.

Like a pencil

In your right hand, hold the hook between your index finger and thumb, with your middle finger underneath to balance and control the hook. Grip the hook just like you would when holding a pencil to write.

If you're a knitter, the chances are you will instinctively hold your crochet hook in the same way that you hold your knitting needle. In both positions, your thumb should be around 5cm (2 in) from the tip of the hook – some crochet hooks will have a special thumb rest located here. When you start, if your stitches are too loose or tight, finding a good position for your crochet hook will help. And if you want to hold your hook in a completely different way to the two methods shown above, go ahead!

Holding the yarn

You will also need to hold the yarn in your left (or free) hand, so you can control the flow and tension. This is called your yarn hand. Most people wrap the yarn around the little finger and lace it through their other fingers, so it ends up over the tip of their forefinger. Here are two different methods for you to try - the forefinger method and the middle finger method. Again, try both of them and settle on the one that feels most comfortable for you.

Forefinger method

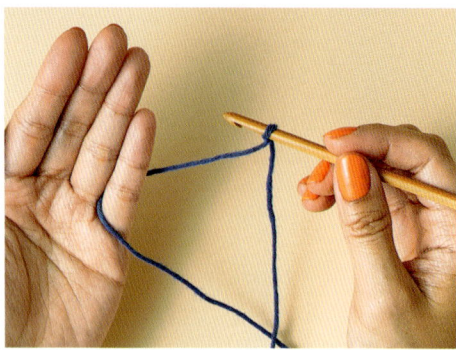

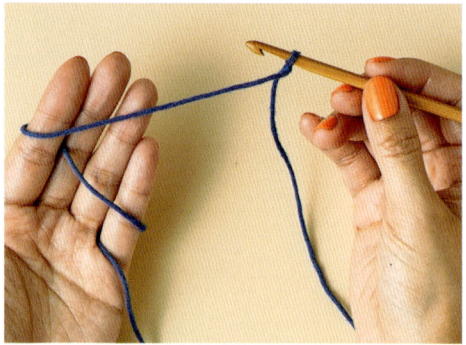

One: Hold the hook with the slip knot in your right hand. With palm upwards, take the working yarn (the end attached to the ball) between the little finger and the next finger and wrap it clockwise around your little finger.

Two: Take the yarn across the next two fingers, then behind and around your index finger.

Three: Hold the yarn, beneath the slip knot, between the thumb and middle finger of your left hand. Now raise your index finger. You are ready to crochet, working with the yarn between the hook and your index finger.

Crochet Essentials

Tensioning the yarn

You do have to apply some tension to the tail end of the yarn, otherwise you will find yourself attempting to crochet in mid air. Depending on the method you're using to control the working yarn, use either the second or third finger and thumb of your left hand to pull gently on the tail end of the yarn by pinching it just below the hook to control your project and stop it from wobbling around too much. I use my index finger a bit like a claw to tension the yarn. It's not the most elegant approach, but it works for me!

Middle finger method

One: Follow step one of the Forefinger method (see opposite), then take the yarn behind your other fingers and round, in front of your index finger.

Two: Hold the yarn between the thumb and forefinger of your left hand. Raise your middle finger to control the yarn. You will work the yarn between the hook and your middle finger.

Making a slip knot

Almost every project starts with a slip knot, which is counted as the first stitch. The slip knot acts as an anchor for the rest of your work.

One: With the yarn end on the right, loop the right side over the left side. Take the yarn end to the back of that loop. Pull the yarn through to make another loop and slide onto your hook.

Two: Pull the yarn tails to tighten the loop, so that the knot sits at the base of the loop on the hook – this is the slip knot. You're now ready to start crocheting.

Crochet Essentials

Making the first loop and working a foundation chain

The first stitch on your hook will be made using a slip knot (see page 37). Once this is on your hook, it's time to get crocheting and to make the first chain of stitches. This first chain is called a foundation chain. The other stitches are then built on top of these foundation chain stitches, so you can create interesting three-dimensional shapes and pieces.

One: With a slip knot on your hook, encircle the working yarn with the hook just above the slip knot in an anticlockwise direction. This is called yarn round hook (yrh) or yarn over (yo) and is used in lots of different crochet techniques.

Two: Holding the base of the slip knot with your yarn hand, with your other hand bring the tip of the hook towards you so that the working yarn is caught in the lip of the hook – if necessary, rotate the hook to hold the yarn in place.

Three: Draw the loop of working yarn through the slip knot already on the hook. This completes your first chain stitch.

Four: Repeat this process, encircling the yarn with the hook and drawing a loop through the loop already on the hook, for each new stitch. Move the fingers of your yarn hand along the foundation chain as you work to maintain the tension. Continue until you have the number of chain stitches you need. When working in rows, this is called the foundation chain. When joined into a ring for working in rounds, this is called the foundation ring.

Counting chain stitches

When working from any pattern, you will need to make a specific number of chains to create the foundation row or ring. To count the chains accurately, it's crucial to be able to recognise the formation of each chain.

The front of a chain

The front of a foundation chain looks like a series of V shapes, each made by the working yarn. Each V is one chain loop, which is smooth on the front side. It is best to count the chains from this front side whenever possible.

The reverse of a chain

The reverse side of the foundation chain is made up by a row of bumps, which sit behind the V shapes on the front side and run vertically from the slip knot to the hook. These are called the back bumps. Whereas the front side is smooth, the reverse side is more textured.

Counting chains

Begin counting the chains from the base of the hook downwards. Do not count the loop on the hook as, at all times, a loop remains on the hook right up the point when you fasten off. I find the easiest way to count stitches is by counting the Vs on the front side to determine the number of chains. Before you start working your pattern beyond the foundation chain or foundation ring, count the chains again to make sure you have exactly the right number.

Basic stitches →

There are just five basic stitches used in crochet which can be combined to make a wide array of shapes, patterns and textures. They range from simple slip stitch up to quadruple trebles, their height increasing in stages depending on the number of times the yarn is wrapped around the hook and drawn through. Don't be confused if you find the same name used for different stitches – UK and U.S. patterns use alternative terminology, so always check the origin of any pattern before you start work, and check the alternative names on the following pages.

Slip stitch (sl)

This is a shallow and functional stitch. It's possible to work it in rows to make a fabric, but it's mostly used for joining stitches together, such as the beginning and end of rows when working in the round or for decreasing. Use it to add an interesting edging and a fun pop of colour to a piece. Before that, it's the perfect stitch to start with in order to practise holding the hook and controlling the yarn.

One: Make a foundation chain of evenly worked chain stitches to the length required. Not including the loop on the hook, count along to the second stitch from the hook.

Two: Insert the tip of the hook through the second chain from the hook, passing it under only one strand of the chain.

Three: Take the hook under, behind and then over the yarn (yarn round hook – yrh) so the yarn is caught by the lip of the hook.

Four: Holding the base of the foundation chain, draw the yarn back through the two loops now on the hook (the second chain and original active loop on the hook). There is now one loop on the hook. This completes one slip stitch.

Five: Continue working slip stitch by inserting the tip of the hook into the next chain along and repeating steps 3 and 4.

When working any crochet stitch, make sure you slide it up onto the shank of the hook - the thicker part that sits between the lip and the grip (see page 33) - before moving on to the next stitch.

Crochet Essentials

Double crochet (U.S. Single crochet)

This is the easiest crochet stitch to learn – the one everyone should start with. It's a versatile and dense stitch, which can be used either on its own or in combination with other stitches. Once you have mastered this stitch, the others will come easily! It can be worked in rows, continuous spiral rounds, or joined rounds. It's often used to make toys and accessories because the fabric is quite textured and stiff. The abbreviation for double crochet is dc (U.S. sc).

One: Make a foundation chain of evenly worked chain stitches to the length required. Not including the loop on the hook, count along to the second stitch from the hook. Insert the tip of the hook through the second chain from the hook, passing it under only one strand of the chain.

Two: Take the hook under, behind and then over the yarn (yarn round hook – yrh) so the yarn is caught by the lip.

Three: Holding the base of the foundation chain, draw the yarn back through the first loop on the hook only (the second chain), leaving the new loop and the original active loop on the hook. There are now two loops on the hook.

Four: Take the hook under, behind and then over the yarn (yarn round hook – yrh) so the yarn is caught by the lip.

Five: Draw the yarn back through both loops on the hook (the new loop and the original active loop on the hook) in one smooth, continuous action and allowing the yarn to flow through your fingers while maintaining a constant tension. There is now one loop on the hook. This completes one double crochet stitch.

Six: Continue working double crochet into each chain of the foundation chain by inserting the tip of the hook into the next chain along and repeating steps 2 to 5.

Seven: If you need to work another row of double crochet, turn the work so the working yarn is at the righthand edge. To begin this new row, make one chain stitch for the turning chain (see page 50) that doesn't count as a stitch but brings the work up to the same height as the double crochet stitches that follow. Work each double crochet stitch into both strands of the top of the double crochet stitches below.

Finished stitch: A fabric made up of double crochet stitches looks like this.

Half treble crochet (U.S. Half double crochet)

The half treble crochet is the next stitch up from double crochet in order of stitch heights (it's taller than a double crochet stitch but half the height of a treble crochet stitch). This stitch produces a fairly dense but fluid fabric, which isn't too lacy, and so it can be used for many different projects. It's essentially the same as double crochet, apart from an extra yarn round hook at the beginning of each stitch. The abbreviation for half treble crochet is htr (U.S. hdc).

One: Make a foundation chain of evenly worked chain stitches to the length required. Take the hook under, behind and then over the yarn (yarn round hook – yrh) so the yarn is caught by the lip.

Two: Not including the loop on the hook, insert the tip of the hook through the third chain from the hook, passing the hook under only one strand of the chain. Yarn round hook (yrh) so the yarn is caught by the lip.

Three: Holding the base of the foundation chain, draw the yarn back through the first loop on the hook only (the third chain), leaving the new loop, yrh and original active loop on the hook. There are now three loops on the hook.

Four: Yarn round hook (yrh) so the yarn is caught by the lip.

Five: Draw the yarn back through all three loops on the hook (the new loop, yrh and original active loop on the hook) allowing the yarn to flow through your fingers while maintaining a constant tension. There is now one loop on the hook. This completes one half treble crochet stitch.

Six: Continue working one half treble stitch into each chain of the foundation chain by inserting the tip of the hook into the next chain along and repeating all the steps, remembering to yrh before inserting the hook through the chain.

 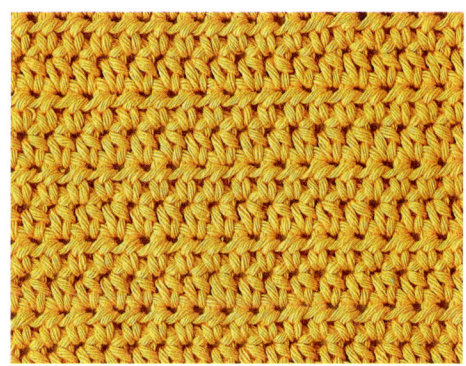

Seven: If you need to work another row of half treble crochet, turn the work so the working yarn is at the righthand edge. To begin this new row, make two chain stitches for the turning chain, which counts as the first half treble stitch of this row. Skip the first stitch at the base of the turning chain, then yrh and work a half treble under both strands of the second stitch in the previous row. Work each half treble crochet stitch into both strands of the top of the half treble crochet stitches in the row below and into the top of the second turning chain of the previous row.

Finished stitch: A fabric made up of half treble crochet stitches looks like this.

Crochet Essentials

Treble crochet (U.S. Double crochet)

Treble crochet is a more open stitch that is twice the height of double crochet. It creates a softer, more fluid fabric that is used in many crochet patterns. Treble crochet is the third of the five basic crochet stitches. You will find that your work grows more quickly with this taller stitch, so it's really satisfying. The abbreviation for treble crochet is tr (U.S. dc).

One: Make a foundation chain of evenly worked chain stitches to the length required. Take the hook under, behind and then over the yarn (yrh or yarn round hook).

Two: Not including the loop on the hook, insert the tip of the hook through the fourth chain from the hook, passing the hook under only one strand of the chain. Yarn round hook (yrh) so the yarn is caught by the lip.

Three: Holding the base of the foundation chain, draw the yarn back through the first loop on the hook only (the fourth chain), leaving the new loop, yrh and original active loop on the hook. There are now three loops on the hook.

Four: Yarn round hook (yrh) so the yarn is caught by the lip. Draw the yarn through the first two loops on the hook, allowing the yarn to flow through your fingers while maintaining a constant tension. There are now two loops on the hook.

Five: Yarn round hook (yrh) so the yarn is caught by the lip. Draw the yarn back through the remaining two loops on the hook. There is now one loop on the hook. This completes one treble crochet stitch.

Six: Continue working one treble stitch into each chain of the foundation row by inserting the tip of the hook into the next chain along and repeating all the steps, remembering to yrh before inserting the hook through the chain.

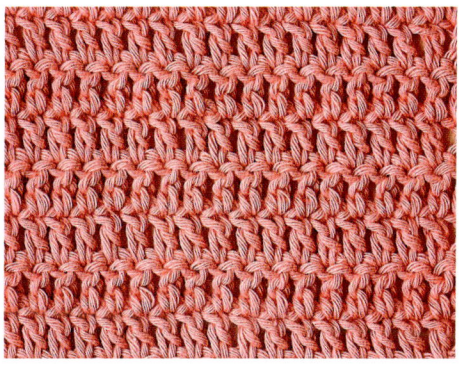

Seven: If you need to work another row of treble crochet, turn the work so the working yarn is at the righthand edge. To begin this new row, make three chain stitches for the turning chain, which counts as the first treble stitch of this row. Skip the first treble crochet stitch at the base of the turning chain, then yrh and work a treble crochet under both strands of the second treble crochet in the previous row. Work each treble crochet into both strands of the top of the treble crochet stitches in the row below, including in the top of the third turning chain of the previous row.

Finished stitch: A fabric made up of treble crochet stitches looks like this.

Double treble crochet (U.S. Triple crochet)

Double treble crochet is an even more open stitch than treble crochet that makes a loose, lacy fabric. Because the stitch is begun by wrapping the yarn around the hook twice, rather than just once, this stitch is a taller version of the treble crochet stitch. It works up really quickly, adding height and detail fast. The abbreviation for double treble crochet is dtr (U.S. trc).

One: Make a foundation chain of evenly worked chain stitches to the length required. Take the hook under, behind and then over the yarn (yarn round hook – yrh) twice.

Two: Not including the loop on the hook, insert the tip of the hook through the fifth chain from the hook, passing the hook under only one strand of the chain. Yarn round hook so the yarn is caught by the lip.

Three: Holding the base of the foundation chain, draw the yarn back through the first loop on the hook only (the fifth chain), leaving the new loop, two yrh and original active loop on the hook. There are now four loops on the hook.

Four: Yarn round hook so the yarn is caught by the lip. Draw the yarn back through the first two loops on the hook, allowing the yarn to flow through your fingers while maintaining a constant tension. There are now three loops on the hook.

Five: Yarn round hook so the yarn is caught by the lip. Draw the yarn back through the first two loops on the hook. There are now two loops on the hook.

Six: Yarn round hook so the yarn is caught by the lip. Draw the yarn back through the remaining two loops on the hook. There is now one loop on the hook. This completes one double treble crochet stitch.

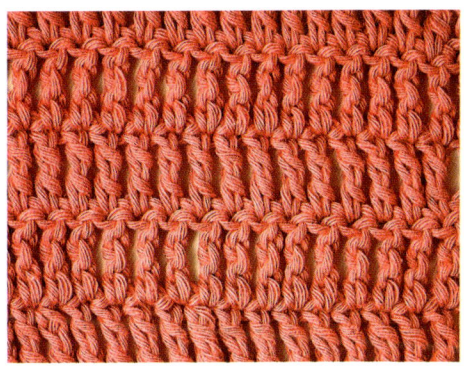

Seven: Work one double treble crochet into each chain of foundation row, remembering to yrh twice before inserting the hook into the chain. To work another row of treble crochet, turn the work so that the working yarn is at the righthand edge. To begin this new row, make four chain stitches for the turning chain, which counts as the first stitch of this row. Skip the first double treble crochet stitch at the base of the turning chain, yrh twice and work a double treble crochet under both strands of the second double treble crochet in the previous row.

Finished stitch: A fabric made up of double treble crochet stitches looks like this.

Working turning chains

To be able to crochet successfully when working in rows, and the work is turned between each row, you must make turning chains before starting the next row of stitches. The turning chain brings the yarn up to the right height to work the first stitch in the next row. The number of chains you need in a turning chain is determined by the height of the basic crochet stitch you're using.

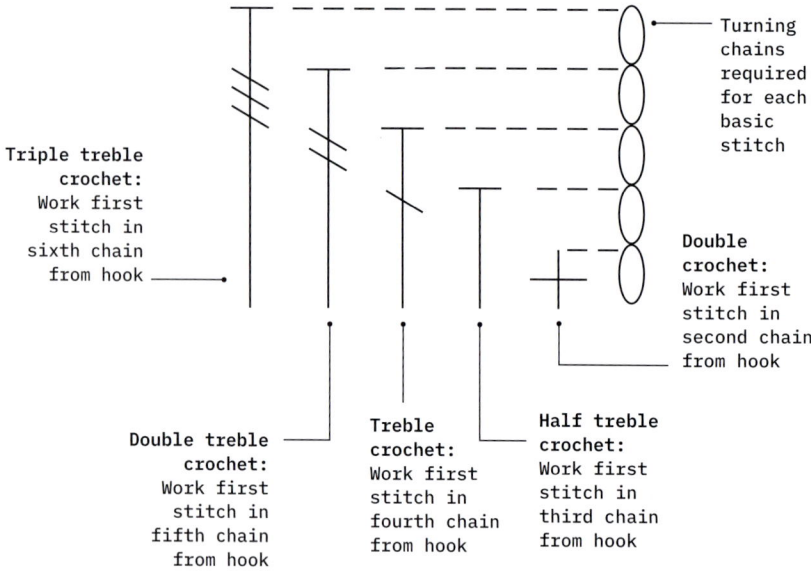

The standard symbols for each of the basic crochet stitches (see page 65) demonstrates the comparative heights of the different stitches. These symbols clearly show how a double treble crochet is much taller than a double crochet, for example. Because the basic crochet stitches vary in height, they required different length turning chains in order to keep the fabric neat and straight. The diagram above highlights the length of turning chain needed to bring the work up to the right height before working a new row of those stitches.

Double crochet
(U.S. Single crochet)
All rows Turning chain of one chain (does not count as a stitch) and insert hook into first stitch of row below.

Half treble crochet
(U.S. Half double crochet)
Foundation row Miss two chains at the beginning of the foundation row.
Following rows Make a turning chain of two chains (does count as first stitch of the row) and insert hook into second stitch of row below. By missing the first stitch you have made the turning chain the first stitch of the new row.

Treble crochet
(U.S. Double crochet)
Foundation row Miss three chains at the beginning of the foundation row.
Following rows Make a turning chain of three chains (does count as first stitch of the row) and insert hook into second stitch of row below. By missing the first stitch you have made the turning chain the first stitch of the new row.

Double treble crochet
(U.S. Triple crochet)
Foundation row Miss four chains at the beginning of the foundation row.
Following rows Make a turning chain of four chains (does count as first stitch of the row) and insert hook into second stitch of row below. By missing the first stitch you have made the turning chain the first stitch of the new row.

Triple treble crochet
(U.S. Double treble crochet)
Foundation row Miss four chains at the beginning of the foundation row.
Following rows Make a turning chain of five chains (does count as first stitch of the row) and insert hook into second stitch of row below. By missing the first stitch you have made the turning chain the first stitch of the new row.

Working in rows
Generally, projects that are flat with straight sides are worked in rows. With rows, you turn your work over from right to left and start another row again, so the end of the previous row sits immediately below the beginning of the next row.

Working in rounds
Both flat and cylindrical shapes are made in the round, by crocheting each round into the top of the previous round, without turning the work. Double crochet stitches (U.S. single crochet stitches) are worked in a continuous spiral without any standing chain – the equivalent of a turning chain. When using any taller stitches, you will need to make standing chains at the beginning of each round to be at the right height to work first stitch. I like the fact that when you are working in the round, you don't have to sew many seams afterwards!

Crochet Essentials

Increasing and decreasing →

There will be patterns that call for increasing (inc) in a row or a round to make the piece wider or decreasing (dec) the number of stitches to make it narrower. The pattern will specify the preferred way to do this as there are a number of different techniques.

CROCHET

Increasing

The most common increases are made by working another stitch (or multiple stitches) into the row you are currently working. Commonly increases are "paired increases" where you increase by one stitch at the beginning of a row and then again at the end of the same row. The technique for increasing at each of a row is shown here on double crochet. With treble crochet and other stitches, the same technique is used – you simply work two stitches into one.

Increasing at the start of a row

One: Make a turning chain of the appropriate height. Here it is double crochet, so that is a turning chain of one chain. Work a full stitch into the correct stitch on the row below, depending on the crochet stitch being worked. As it is double crochet being worked here, that is one double crochet into the first stitch on the row below.

Two: Insert the hook once more into the same stitch on the row below and work a second stitch where the first stitch was just worked. Here, a second double crochet is worked in the same place as the first double crochet. This completes the increase by one stitch at the beginning of the row. Continue working one double crochet, or whatever stitch you are working, in the usual way into each stitch to the end of the row.

Increasing at the end of a row

One: Work to the last stitch in the row below and then, at the end of the row, work a double crochet, or whatever stitch you are working, into this last stitch of the row, but do not turn the row or fasten off.

Two: Insert the hook once again into the same place as the last stitch worked and make a second stitch into the last stitch on the row below. Here, a second double crochet is worked in the same place as the first double crochet. This completes the increase by one stitch at the end of a row.

Crochet Essentials

Decreasing

There are several ways of decreasing stitches. This is slightly trickier than increasing stitches but, in essence, it's about turning two stitches into one. You can simply skip a stitch as you work, although this may leave a hole. It's best to spend a bit of time using one of these decreasing techniques, which have different shaping effects. Decreases can be made at any point along a row (your pattern should tell you where). As with increases, decreases are most frequently worked as pairs at either end of a row, especially for garments. The techniques below show you how to make decreases in double crochet.

Decreasing at the beginning of a row

One: To decrease one stitch at the beginning of a row of double crochet, work up to the last yarn round hook of the first double crochet in the usual way, but do not complete the stitch. There are now two loops on the hook.

Two: Insert the hook through the next stitch and draw a loop through. There are now three loops on the hook.

Three: Wrap the yarn around the hook and draw a loop through all three loops in one go. This completes the decrease. Where there were two stitches, there is now only one.

Decreasing at the end of a row

One: Work to the last two stitches in the row below and then, at the end of the row, insert the hook through the top of the second to last stitch and draw a loop through. There are now two loops on the hook.

Two: Insert the hook through the last stitch in the row below and draw a loop through. There are now three loops on the hook.

TOM'S TIP:

Three: Wrap the yarn round the hook and draw a loop through all three loops in one go. This completes the decrease. Where there were two stitches, there is now only one.

You can use the same principle to make decreases on other stitches, including treble crochet, by making two incomplete stitches up to the last yarn round hook for each stitch and then drawing a loop through both at the same time. You can also decrease more than one stitch at a time in the same way. To make a "double decrease" and turn three stitches into one, work three incomplete double crochet or treble crochet up to the last yarn round hook and join them together at the top with the last yarn round hook.

Crochet Essentials

Stitches every crocheter should know →

When I first started to crochet, I learnt all the basic stitches (see pages 40–49) before experimenting with other crocheted fabrics. But once you have the double crochet and treble crochet techniques under your belt, you can use these two main crochet stitches to create different textures and patterns.

CROCHET

Written instructions are given below for my favourite texture stitch patterns to get you started. Just take things slow, working row by row or round by round, and soon you will see an exciting stitch pattern emerge.

Woven stitch

Sometimes called linen stitch or moss stitch, this combination of stitches creates a textured fabric that is similar to its knitted counterpart. This is a good starter stitch for novice crocheters that results in a solid fabric, but one with more drape than double crochet (U.S. single crochet) and a subtle all-over texture, which is also reversible. It is made by working double crochet and chains alternately, and then working double crochets in the chain spaces of the preceding row with chains between them.

Make a foundation chain with an even number of chains.
Row 1: 1dc in 2nd chain from hook, * 1ch, miss 1 ch, 1dc in next chain, repeat from * to end, turn.
Row 2: 1ch (does not count as a stitch), 1dc in 1st dc, 1dc in next 1-chain space, * 1ch, 1dc in next 1-chain space, repeat from * to last dc, 1dc in last dc, turn.
Row 3: 1ch (does not count as a stitch), 1dc in 1st dc, * 1ch, 1dc in next 1-chain space; repeat from * to last 2 dc, 1ch, miss 1 dc, 1dc in last dc, turn.
Repeat Rows 2 and 3 to form pattern.

Rope stitch

Made by working a V-shape combination of two treble crochet (U.S. double crochet) and 1 chain into each chain space on the row below, this simple rope stitch makes a fluid fabric that is perfect for blankets and throws. Because the rope stitch is quite open, with lots of spaces between stitches, it traps warm air and makes a lovely snugly blanket.

Make a foundation chain with a multiple of three chains.
Row 1: 1tr in 4th chain from hook, 1ch, 1tr in next chain, * miss 1 chain, 1tr in next chain, 1ch, 1tr in next chain, repeat from * to last chain, 1tr in last chain at end, turn.
Row 2: 3ch (counts as first tr), work (1tr, 1ch, 1tr) all in each 1-chain space to end of row, 1tr in top of 3-chain at end, turn.
Repeat Row 2 to form pattern.

Crochet Essentials

Bobble stitch

Bobble stitches are really cute and add a fun element to crochet projects. Basically, bobbles are made by working lots of treble crochet together in the same stitch until they "pop" out of your work on the wrong side. You can place bobbles next to each other, as here, or you can spread them apart and position them wherever you fancy.

Here is the technique for making a bobble:
1 bobble = (yrh, insert hook in stitch, yrh, draw loop through, yrh, draw loop through first 2 loops on hook) 5 times all in same stitch, yrh, draw loop through all 6 loops on hook.

Make a foundation chain with an uneven number of chains.
Row 1: 1dc in 2nd chain from hook, dc to end of row, turn.
Row 2: 1ch, *1dc in 1st st, 1 bobble in next st, rep from * to last st, 1dc in next st, turn.
Row 3: 1ch, 1dc in 1st st, dc to end of row, turn.
Row 4: 1 bobble in 1st st, *1dc in next st, 1 bobble in next st, rep from * to last 2 sts, 1dc in each of last 2 sts, turn.
Row 5: Work as Row 3.
Repeat Rows 2 to 5 to form pattern, finishing with a Row 3.

Loop stitch

The loop stitch is a versatile way to add texture to a crochet project and looks brilliant on loads of different items. The loops can be made as big or as small as you like by adjusting the position of your tension finger. For a smaller loop you can use a pencil or for a longer loop you can use two fingers. You can even trim the loops for a slightly different effect.

Here is the technique for making a loop:
1 loop st = insert hook in stitch, wrap yarn around index finger held at preferred length for loop, wrap hook clockwise around yarn in front of index finger, catch yarn laying behind index finger, pull yarn through stitch (two loops on hook), yarn over, pull through remaining loops, remove finger from loop.

Make a foundation chain with the preferred number of chains plus 1 chain for turning.
Row 1: 1dc in 2nd chain from hook, dc to end of row, turn.
Row 2: 1ch (does not count as stitch), 1 loop st in each st to end of row, turn.
Row 3: 1dc in 1st st, dc to end of row, turn.
Repeat Rows 2 and 3 to form pattern, finishing with a Row 2.

Treble crochet square

Note: Do not turn at the end of rounds but continue with the right side of the motif always facing.

Foundation ring: Make 4ch and join with a slip stitch to 1st chain to form a ring.
Round 1 (RS): 5ch (counts as 1tr and 2-chain space), [3tr in ring, 2ch] 3 times, 2tr in ring, join with a slip stitch to 3rd of 5-chain at beg of round. *3tr along each side of square.*
Round 2: Work 1 slip stitch in 1st space, 7ch (counts as 1tr and 4-chain space), 2tr in same sp, *1tr in each tr to next space, work (2tr, 4ch, 2tr) all in next space, repeat from * twice more, 1tr in each tr to next space, 1tr in same space as 7-chain, join with a slip stitch to 3rd of 7-chain at beg of round. *7tr along each side of square.*
Round 3: Repeat Round 2. *11 tr along each side of square.*
Round 4: Repeat Round 2. *15 tr along each side of square.*

Treble crochet hexagon

Note: Do not turn at the end of rounds but continue with the right side of the motif always facing.

Foundation ring: Make 4ch and join with a slip stitch to 1st chain to form a ring.
Round 1 (RS): 3ch (counts as 1st tr), 1tr in ring, (1ch, 2tr in ring) 5 times, 1ch, join with a slip stitch to top of 3-chain at beg of round.
Round 2: Work 1 slip stitch in 1st tr, 1 slip stitch in next chain, 3ch (counts as 1st tr), *1tr in each of next 2tr, work (1tr, 1ch, 1tr) in next 1-chain space, repeat from * 4 times more, 1tr in each of next 2tr, 1tr in last 1-chain space, 1ch, join with a slip stitch to top of 3-chain at beg of round.
Round 3: 3ch (counts as 1st tr), 1tr in each tr to 1st 1-chain space, work (1tr, 1ch, 1tr) in 1st 1-chain space, * 1tr in each tr to next 1-chain space, work (1tr, 1ch, 1tr) in next 1-chain space, repeat from * to end, join with a slip stitch to top of 3-chain at beg of round.
Rounds 4 and 5: Repeat Round 3 twice.

Reading a crochet pattern →

A crochet pattern will include the same details as a knitting pattern, including the skill level, materials needed, recommended tension, and instructions for working your crocheted fabric. Patterns can look daunting at first, but once you get started and you begin to recognise the frequently used abbreviations, it will all make perfect sense.

Understanding crochet abbreviations

Crochet abbreviations make what could be a very long piece of text much shorter. Generally, each pattern will also include any specific abbreviations. Understanding this shorthand will help you read any crochet pattern.

UK and U.S. terminology
Depending on the nationality of the designer, crochet patterns can be written using either UK or U.S. terms. Although I am British, I learnt the U.S. terms first because I watched a lot of online tutorials by American designers. However, in this book I always give the UK term first with the U.S. term following in brackets. I know this part is a bit confusing, but it's vitally important to know what terminology the pattern is using and what stitch you are required to work.

General
Instructions are written using UK terminology with the U.S. terminology given in round brackets ( ) afterwards

[ ] instructions are given for the smallest size first, with changes for the larger sizes given in order within square brackets afterwards

( ) work any instructions within round brackets as many times as directed afterwards

* repeat instructions following the single asterisk as many times as directed afterwards

** repeat instructions between asterisks as many times as directed or from a given set of instructions

alt alternate
approx. approximately
beg begin or beginning
cc contrasting colour
ch(s) chain(s)
ch-sp chain space
cm centimetres
cont continue
dc double crochet (U.S. single crochet)
dc2tog double crochet two stitches together (U.S. single crochet two stitches together)
dec decrease or decreasing
dk double knitting (U.S. light worsted weight)
dtr double treble crochet (U.S. treble crochet)
foll follow(s) or following
g grams
htr half treble crochet (U.S. half double crochet)
htr2tog half treble two stitches together (U.S. half double crochet two stitches together)
in inch(es)
inc increase or increasing
lp(s) loop(s)
m metres
meas measures
mc main colour
miss skip
mm millimetres
oz ounces
patt(s) pattern(s)
pm place marker
qtr quadruple treble crochet (U.S. triple treble crochet)
quintr quintuple treble crochet

rem remain or remaining
rep repeat or repeating
rnd(s) round(s)
RS right side
sl st slip stitch
sm slip marker
sp(s) space(s)
ss slip stitch
st(s) stitch(es)
tbl through back loop
tch turning chain
tfl through front loop
tog together
tr treble crochet (U.S. double crochet)
tr2tog treble two stitches together
trtr triple treble crochet (U.S. double treble)
WS wrong side
yrh yarn round hook

Reading a crochet pattern

Most patterns will be split into different parts, so just tackle each one at a time. I always tick off what I have done as I go. Make the pieces in the order given in the instructions, whether it's a garment, toy or something else, and take it all one step at a time. Work along each row or round bit by bit, rather than trying to read the entire instruction and then complete the row or round without referring back.

Most commercial crochet patterns follow this format:

1 Skill level: Some patterns state the skill level needed, so beginners are able to practise basic crochet stitches, shaping and colourwork. As a beginner, I advise looking for small items like the Friendship Bracelets on pages 84–87 that are quick to make and relatively easy in order to build confidence. The first item I completed was a hat for my son, Robbie. You could try the Bucket Hat on pages 98–101 to practise making motifs and some other simple stitches.

2 Measurements: If the pattern is for a garment, usually a range of sizes are given. Based on the measurements given, choose which size you want to make and follow that throughout the instructions. Otherwise, if a project is one-size, like a cushion, then the finished dimensions are stated.

3 What you will need: This tells you the type of yarn, the standard yarn weight, the meterage (yardage) and the number of balls needed. Always try to use the yarn specified by the pattern designer, but if you cannot source that particular yarn, choose a suitable substitute yarn (see page 28). It will also tell you anything else you need to complete the project, like stitch markers.

4 Tension (gauge): This is the number of stitches and rows contained in a certain area, usually a 10cm (4 in) square. Always work a tension (gauge) swatch before starting to crochet any project and change the hook size if necessary to achieve the recommended tension.

5 Abbreviations: This will give you a key to all of the shorthand abbreviations used within the pattern.

6 Pattern instructions: This is either written out line by line or presented in chart form with a key alongside to decode the chart. Designers will aim to give you the right tips and information to make your work a success. Instructions for a crochet project will always start with the number of chains needed for the foundation chain.

7 Finishing instructions: This will tell you how to finish off the project, including what seaming techniques to use when joining pieces together.

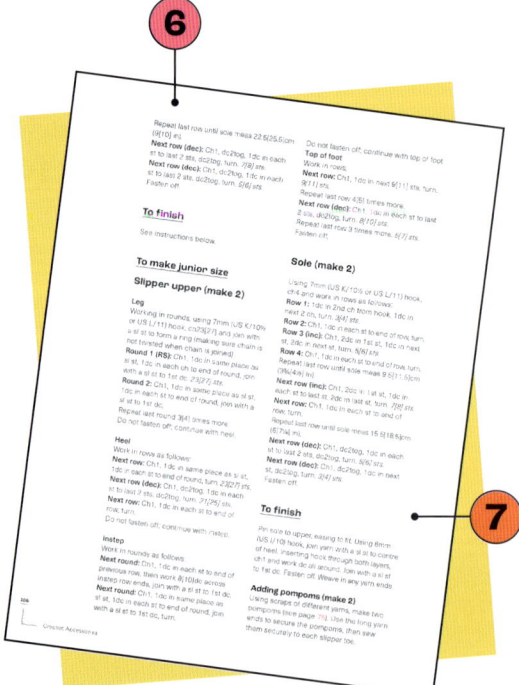

Crochet Essentials

Cosy Slippers

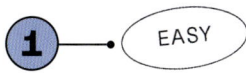 EASY

The first thing I do when I get home is kick off my shoes and get cosy in my slippers. This boot-style version is stylish and soft, crocheted in super chunky 100% merino wool, to keep toes and ankles toasty. Quick to make for you and for the whole family, with a junior size, then get creative and customise with stripes and pompoms.

Measurements

Adult size	M	L	
Foot length	24.5	27.5	cm
	9½	11	in

Junior size	XS	S	
Foot length	18.5	21.5	cm
	7¼	8½	in

What you will need
- Wool Couture Cheeky Chunky 100% merino wool, 65m (71 yards) per 100g (3½ oz)

ADULT SIZE Quantity:
- **A** 3 x 100g (3½ oz) balls in Aquamarine
- **B** 1 x 100g (3½ oz) ball in Black
- **C** 1 x 100g (3½ oz) ball in Aqua
- **D** 1 x 100g (3½ oz) ball in Mustard
- **E** 1 x 100g (3½ oz) ball in Raspberry
- **F** 1 x 100g (3½ oz) ball in Natural Cream

JUNIOR SIZE Quantity:
- 2 x 100g (3½ oz) balls in Raspberry
- Scraps in random colours, for pompoms
- 6mm (US J/10) crochet hook
- 7mm (US K/10½ or US L/11) crochet hook
- Yarn needle

Tension (gauge)
10 sts and 12 rows to 10cm (4 in) over dc using 7mm (US K/10½ or US L/11) hook, or size required to achieve the correct tension (gauge).

Abbreviations
See page 61.
dc2tog (insert hook in next st, yrh and draw loop through) twice, yrh and draw through all 3 loops on hook. One stitch decreased.

Special techniques
Changing colour at the end of a row (see page 107).
Making pompoms (see page 75).

Note
The slippers are made in two separate pieces – the upper and the sole.

Working from a chart

Depending on the project, your crochet pattern may come with a colour chart or stitch diagram, as well as written instructions. Being able to decipher these charts and diagrams and understand what each symbol denotes, means that you can crochet in any language. As they give an immediate visual impression of what the finished piece will look like, they are great for people who are really visual learners.

Crochet charts

Charts in the form of a grid are used alongside written patterns, especially where colourwork or filet crochet is better represented as a visual image. In these charts, each square represents a stitch or group of stitches. It will show you what colours are used for certain stitches or a block of stitches and how they are placed in relation to each other, so you can visualise the overall effect in your piece. When a colour or stitch pattern is repeated several times across a row, often only the repeated section is charted, plus any extra stitches at the start and end of the rows. The pattern repeat is clearly indicated, usually by a line pointing to the repeated stitches. These stitches are worked across the rows as many times as needed, while those stitches outside the repeat are worked just once either at the start or end of the row.

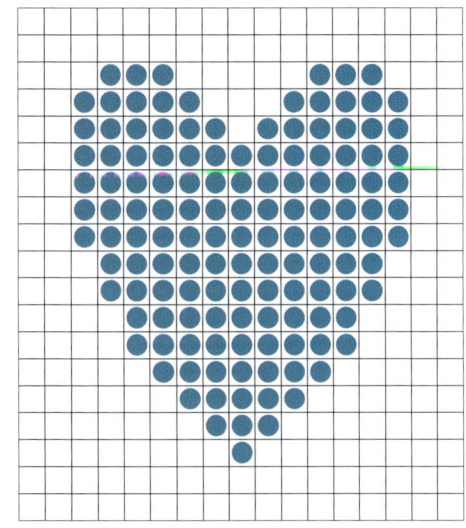

Key: ☐ work open mesh
      ● work solid block

Filet crochet chart and key

Crochet stitch diagrams
Crochet patterns may be conveyed in the form of diagrams. Made up of a series of symbols used to represent stitches, they imitate the size and shape of the actual stitch. Each row or round will have a number so you know which direction you're working in and stitches will be shown in relative sizes, to give you a good idea of how the pattern will look. They are particularly useful because you are able to see where to work each stitch.

Working in rows from a stitch diagram
When working in rows, start in the bottom lefthand corner with the foundation chain, then follow the row numbers from the bottom of the diagram to the top. Usually, odd-numbered rows run from right to left and even-numbered rows run from left to right. Each row may be linked with a turning chain.

Working in rounds from a stitch diagram
When working in the round, you generally work from the centre outwards. Each round is numbered, so follow the ascending row numbers outwards in concentric circles. They are designed for right-handed crocheters; left-handed crocheters will need to work from the chart as a mirror image.

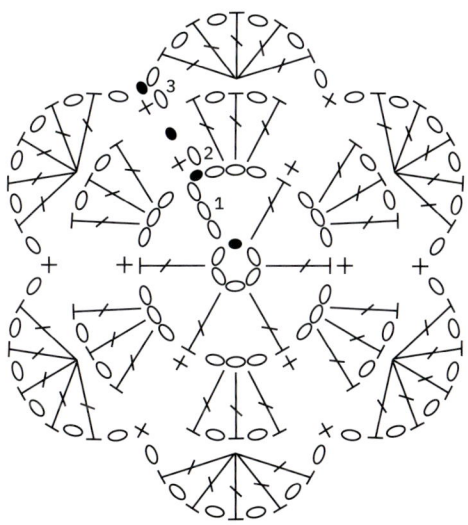

Key:
○ chain
● slip stitch
+ double crochet
⊤ treble crochet

5 treble crochet in same stitch

Crochet Essentials

Working a tension or gauge swatch

It is really important to get into the habit of completing a tension or gauge swatch for every project that you're about to embark on, so the final size of your finished project is correct. We all crochet slightly differently - some tighter, some looser - so you may need to adjust how much tension you apply to the working yarn or change the size of the hook you are using in order to achieve the same size stitches as the pattern designer intended. I know working a tension swatch may seem a bit tedious, but what is far worse is to get to the end of a project only to find out that it does not fit!

If the pattern states the number of stitches and rows measured over a 10cm (4 in) square, always work a tension swatch at least a few centimetres (an inch) extra as often the side stitches can be a little tighter than the main fabric, so you can take your measurement from the middle of the swatch.

Lay your swatch flat or block it without stretching it. Measure out 10cm (4 in) across the centre with a ruler or tape measure and mark with pins. Count the number of stitches between the pins and jot that number down. Count the number of rows in the same way. If the number of stitches and rows meets the number stated in the pattern, then great! If not, you may need to go up a hook size if you crochet with a tight tension, or down a hook size, if you are a loose crocheter. Work the swatch again to check you are on track, then use the size of hook that best matches the recommended tension. Every crocheter's work is different, so every garment will end up looking and fitting slightly differently.

TOM'S TIP:

When you have lots of crochet tension swatches, put them to good use and re-purpose them into something useful. Depending on the fibre of the yarn, they can make great coasters around the house. Or embroider each one with an initial and give them as gifts.

Troubleshooting tips →

Whether you're just starting out or have years of crochet experience, there will always be times when your crocheting doesn't quite go to plan. Here are some of the most common mistakes and how you can fix them. When I first started, I made every single one of these mistakes (many times over).

Wrong tension or gauge

When I started crocheting, I found one of the hardest things to achieve was getting the correct tension. When your tension is too slack, this results in looser stitches and possibly holes, whereas if it is too tight, it can be hard to insert the hook into the chains and the resulting fabric can be too stiff. Always practise new stitches on a tension (gauge) swatch – it helps with getting the technique down and sorting your tension. I think it's a case of finding a comfortable finger position holding the yarn and then practise, practise, practise.

Crocheting through the front loop only

When you are starting out, it is easy to crochet through the front loop only and then wonder why your crochet fabric does not look quite right. Some patterns may call for this technique but if not, be sure you are counting your stitches and that you work into every stitch.

The best way to recognise if you have been doing this is when the front and back of your crochet look slightly different or if your piece has grown larger than expected. Make sure that you go under both front and back loops.

TOM'S TIP:

```
If it's your foundation chain that
is too loose or too tight, try this:
If your chain is too tight, try a
hook that is one size larger than
the pattern calls for and then switch
back to the recommended size for the
first row or round. If your chain is
too loose, go down a hook size to make
your foundation chain.
```

Your project is getting wider

If your crochet is growing in width, don't panic – we've all been there! If this happens, it means you are gaining some extra stitches along the way. It is really important to count and keep track of your rows and stitches. There are cool little row counters that you can put on your finger, which you adjust each time you complete a row. There are also stitch markers to mark the first and last stitch of the row. I do the same as I do with knitting and put my stitch markers in every 10 rows. If I am working in the round, I put in a stitch marker at the beginning of each new round.

Finishing your makes →

You've now finished crocheting your project – congrats! After spending time creating something beautiful, the last thing you want is for it to unravel and so you must take the time to finish the piece off properly. Don't leave anything to chance!

CROCHET

Fastening off

Once you've finished crocheting any piece, you need to fasten off securely, so the stitches do not unravel. Fastening off is incredibly simple as there will be only one loop left on your hook at the end of your work.

One: Complete the final row or round so that you're left with one loop on the hook. Cut the yarn at approx. 30cm (12 in) from the hook. Wrap the cut yarn around the hook and draw it through the last remaining loop on the hook.

Two: Slide the hook out of the loop and bring the yarn end through the loop. Gently pull on the yarn end to tighten the knot and secure the stitch.

Weaving in yarn ends

I prefer to work over any yarn ends that are the result of changing colour or adding in a new ball of yarn as I crochet, so there is less weaving in to do at the end of a project. It depends on what the pattern calls for, however, and there's always the very last yarn end to deal with after fastening off.

One: To disguise any yarn ends that have not already been "enclosed" by working over them, thread the yarn end through a yarn needle and neatly weave the yarn through six or more stitches on the wrong side of the work.

Two: Carefully snip the yarn end close to the crochet fabric, making sure you do not cut the fabric itself.

Crochet Essentials

Crochet seaming methods

When piecing together a crocheted garment or any other project, use the seaming method described in the pattern, if specified. Before sewing up your creation, block each piece carefully by either steam blocking or spray blocking. Always sew seams with the same yarn used to crochet the fabric, threaded through a blunt-tipped sewing needle.

Backstitch seam — Resulting in a sturdy seam, joining pieces with backstitch is the best method to use for sewing together items like bags and toys.

One: Line up the crochet pieces side by side, with their wrong sides facing upwards, and secure the yarn with a few oversew stitches made in the same spot.

Two: Insert the needle through the edges of both pieces, taking the yarn forward by two crochet stitches.

Three: Next, take the yarn backwards by one stitch. On the backwards stitch, be sure to insert the needle in the same place as the end of the last backwards stitch.

Four: Continue to the end of the seam. Secure the yarn to fasten off.

Mattress stitch seam

This is my favourite method of seaming pieces as it creates the neatest flat seam. You can use it on crochet fabric made up of any stitch.

One: Lay the pieces side by side with right sides upwards. Bring the needle up at the left corner of the righthand piece. Make a double stitch across to the right corner of the other piece.

Two: Take the needle up half-way through the first stitch on the left edge.

Three: Make the next stitch along the centre of the crochet stitch or turning chain at the edge of the righthand piece.

Four: Make the next stitch in the same way, working along one crochet stitch or turning chain on the lefthand piece.

Five: Continue along the seam, alternating between the righthand and lefthand pieces, taking a stitch on each side.

Six: After every few stitches, pull the sewing yarn taut so that the seam stitches disappear and are no longer visible on the right side of the crochet.

Whip stitch seam

This seaming method, which is sometimes called an overcast stitch seam, is one of the quickest ways to join your crochet pieces together. It's virtually invisible and creates a strong join.

One: Thread a blunt-tipped sewing needle with a length of yarn that is around two or three times the length of the edges you are seaming. Place the two crochet pieces with their right sides together and secure the yarn with a few oversew stitches in the same spot.

Two: Starting at the righthand edge, join pairs of crochet stitches by sliding the needle through all four loops. Bring the yarn needle in the same direction with each stitch. Do not overtighten.

Three: Repeat until you have sewn through the back loops of all pairs of crochet stitches. When you reach the final corner, fasten off and weave in the yarn end.

Four: An alternative way to work this discreet seam is to pick up just the outside loops of each stitch.

Making pompoms

Who doesn't love a pompom? They bring such joy and they're a great way to use up scraps of yarn. They're really easy to make, either with a store-bought pompom maker or in the traditional way with two circles cut from stiff cardboard, slightly wider in diameter than the finished size of the pompom with a hole in the centre of each, measuring just under half the diameter.

One: If you're using a pompom maker, open out the two parts and hold them together. Wind two yarns along each half in turn until the semi-circular gap is filled, then fasten the catches. If you're using cardboard, thread a large-eyed needle with two long strands of yarn. Holding the circles together, stitch the yarn continually through the centre and around the outer edges, keeping the strands close together, until the centre space is almost filled.

Two: Insert the tip of sharp scissors between the two sides of the pompom maker or two cardboard circles and snip through the layers of yarn all around the edge.

Three: Slip a length of yarn through the centre space and wrap it tightly around the yarn strands. This will be the centre of the pompom. Firmly knot the yarn, leaving long ends that can later be used to attach the pompom. Remove the pompom maker or cardboard circles.

Four: Fluff up the pompom and trim any uneven strands of yarn sticking out for a neat, round finish.

Crochet Accessor

-03

es

EASY

Kit Bag

When I'm training, I live out of a kit bag, so I decided to crochet one. Based on the classic cylindrical sports bag and made a little more on-trend in stripes of tonal colours, simply crochet a wide rectangle and two circles, then sew in a zip to create a practical bag. Perfect for heading to the gym, the beach, or the armchair with your latest project.

Measurements
Approx. 50cm (19¾in) long and 27cm (10¾in) diameter, excluding handles

What you will need
- Rico Essentials Cotton DK
  100% cotton, 120m (131 yards) per 50g (1¾ oz)
- **A** 3 x 50g (1¾ oz) balls in Dark Teal (40)
- **B** 10 x 50g (1¾ oz) balls in Red (02)
- **C** 3 x 50g (1¾ oz) balls in Pumpkin (87)
- **D** 2 x 50g (1¾ oz) balls in Alga (73)
- **E** 1 x 50g (1¾ oz) ball in Banana (63)
- **F** 2 x 50g (1¾ oz) balls in Black (90)
- 3.5mm (US E/4) crochet hook
- 4mm (US G/6) crochet hook
- 1 zipper, 48cm (19 inches) long
- Yarn needle
- Sewing needle

Tension (gauge)
21 sts and 25 rows to 10cm (4in) over dc using 4mm (US G/6) hook, or size required to achieve the correct tension (gauge).

Abbreviations
See page 61.

Special techniques
Working in the round (see pages 82–83).

Notes
When instructed to switch colours, do this on last stitch of current colour as follows: insert hook in last stitch of current colour, yarn around hook with current colour and pull loop through, drop current colour, pick up next colour, yarn around hook with next colour and pull through both loops to complete the dc. Next colour is now on the hook.

Crochet Accessories

To make

Body of bag

Using 4mm (US G/6) hook and **A**, ch122, change to **B** and ch46, turn.
Row 1 (RS): Starting in 2nd st from hook and using **B**, work 45dc switching to **A** at colour change (see Notes on page 79), work 122dc to end, ch1 (does not count as a st throughout), turn. *167 sts.*
Row 2: Starting in 2nd st from hook and using **A**, work 122dc switching to **B** at colour change on previous row, work 45dc to end, ch1, turn.
Rows 3 to 6: Repeat Rows 1 and 2 twice.
Rows 7 to 12: Replacing **A** with **C**, repeat Rows 1 to 6.
Rows 13 to 24: Replacing **B** with **D**, repeat Rows 1 to 12.
Rows 1 to 24 set colour sequence of 6 rows **A** and **B**, 6 rows **C** and **B**, 6 rows **A** and **D** and 6 rows **C** and **D**.
Rows 25 to 120: Repeat Rows 1 to 24 four times, following colour sequence as set.
At end of last row of **C** and **D**, omit final ch1. Cut yarn and draw end through to fasten off.

Zipper edge

With RS facing, using 4mm (US G/6) hook, join **E** to right-most st on one short edge of bag body and ch1.
Row 1 (RS): Work dc along this short edge of bag body using **E**, working into the end of each row, ch1, turn. *120 sts.*
Row 2: Starting in 2nd st from hook, work 1dc in each st to end, ch1, turn.
Row 3: Starting in 2nd st from hook, work 1dc in each st to end, cut yarn and draw end through to fasten off.

Circular ends (make two)

Make one circular end using **A** and **D** and another using **B** and **C**, alternating colours after every 5 rounds.
Using 4mm (US G/6) hook and either **A** or **B**, ch4, slip st in 1st ch to form a ring.
Round 1 (RS): Ch1 (does not count as a st), 6dc into ring. *6dc.*
Cont working in a spiral without joining each round.
Round 2: 2dc in each st. *12dc.*
Round 3: [1dc, 2dc in next st] 6 times. *18dc.*
Round 4: [2dc, 2dc in next st] 6 times. *24dc.*
Round 5: [3dc, 2dc in next st] 6 times, switching to next colour (either **D** or **C**) on last yrh of last dc. *30dc.*
Cont in this way, alternating colours after 5 rounds, and on subsequent round working 1 additional dc, before working increase. Always work increase [2dc in next st] in 2nd dc of 2dc increase on previous round.
Work until diameter meas 27cm (10¾ in). Cut yarn and draw end through to fasten off.

Handles (make two)

Using 3.5mm (US E/4) hook and **F**, ch9, turn.
Row 1 (RS): Starting in 2nd st from hook, 8dc, ch1, turn. *8dc.*
Rows 2 to 56: Cont in **F** and work 55 rows in dc starting in 2nd st from hook and finishing with a ch1, turn. On Row 56, before working the final ch1, switch to **E** on last dc of row (see Notes on page 79), ch1, turn.
Rows 57 to 65: Using **E**, work 9 rows in dc starting in 2nd st from hook and finishing with a ch1 as before. On Row 65, before working the final ch1, switch to **F** on last dc of row (see Notes on page 79), ch1, turn.
Rows 66 to 130: Using **F**, work 65 rows in dc starting in 2nd st from hook and finishing with a ch1 as before. On Row 130, before working the final ch1, switch to **E** on last dc of row (see Notes on page 79), ch1, turn.
Rows 131 to 160: Using **E**, work 30 rows in dc starting in 2nd st from hook and finishing with a ch1 as before. On Row 160, before working the final ch1, switch to **F** on last dc of row (see Notes on page 79), ch1, turn.
Rows 161 to 225: Using **F**, work 65 rows in dc starting in 2nd st from hook and finishing with a ch1 as before. On Row 225, before working the final ch1, switch to **E** on last dc of row, ch1, turn.

Rows 226 to 234: Using **E**, work 9 rows in dc starting in 2nd st from hook and finishing with a ch1 as before. On Row 234, before working the final ch1, switch to **F** on last dc of row, ch1, turn.

Rows 235 to 289: Using **F**, work 55 rows in dc starting in 2nd st from hook and finishing with a ch1, turn.

Final row: Starting in 2nd st from hook, 1dc in each st to end, cut yarn and draw end through to fasten off.

To finish

Weave in any yarn ends.
Stitch zipper in place, centred along **E** edges of bag body, using **E** and neat backstitch.
At one end of zipper, stitch edges of crochet together for 2cm (¾ in) using whip stitch. Repeat at other end of zipper.
Use 4mm (US G/6) hook to attach circular ends to long edges of bag body using **C** for **B** and **C** circle and **A** for **A** and **D** circle as follows: Make a slipknot on hook. Working from right side of work, insert hook through edge stitches of both pieces of bag body and circular end, and join yarn with a sl st. Ch1 (does not count as a st) and work dc all around, working through both layers, join with a sl st to 1st dc and fasten off. (Use pins to keep your work in position before crocheting to achieve an even seam without stretching or puckering.)
Stitch handles in position, short edges meeting on bottom centre of bag body. Use backstitch and change cotton colour from **F** to **E** to match crochet being stitched down.

Crochet Accessories

Masterclass

Working in the round

The ends of this kit bag are circular. Rather than being worked backwards and forwards in horizontal rows, you make a central ring and continue working outwards in a circle. When working in rounds, the right side of the work is facing you at all times. The shape of the circle is created by the increases that are made as you work in the round.

Instead of joining the first and last stitches of each round with a slip stitch, these circular bag ends are worked in a spiral, with the first stitch of each round being worked into the first stitch of the previous round, so you don't really see where one round ends and another begins. The downside of working in a spiral this way is that the finished circular piece will end with a small bump where the stitches are fastened off – but this bump will disappear into the seam of the bag once it is made up, so it's no big deal.

One   Work the required number of chains for the short foundation chain – here it is six chains. Insert the hook into the first chain made (that is furthest away from the hook), wrap the yarn round the hook and draw a loop through the chain and the loop on the hook to close the ring with a slip stitch.

Two   Work a standing chain for the first round. The number of chains worked for this standing chain depends on the stitch being used. For double crochet, as shown here, it is one chain. For treble crochet it would be three chains. Except for double crochet, this counts as the first stitch.

Three   Now work each stitch of the first round as instructed in the pattern. Work the stitches into the centre of the ring by inserting the hook into the space and not into the loops of the foundation ring. While working the first round of stitches, lay the yarn end around the top of the chain so the yarn tail is covered by the stitches being worked.

Four   The last stitch of the first round should be made in the last stitch of the foundation ring. When all the double crochet stitches of the first round are complete, mark the last stitch of the round with a stitch marker – here it is the sixth stitch. Pull the yarn tail to close the centre hole and clip it off close to the crochet stitches.

Five   Start the second round by working into the next available stitch, which should be the first stitch of the first round. For this second round, work 2 double crochet into each double crochet stitch, as instructed in the pattern. The last stitch of the second round should be made in the stitch just to the right of the stitch marker.

TOM'S TIP: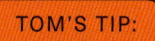

Stitch markers are your friend when working in the round. Because it's not always that easy to determine where a new round starts, keep moving the stitch marker each time to identify the last stitch in each round, until your piece is the size required. The number of stitches in each round increases as the circle of stitches grows in size, but the last stitch will always be at the same point.

Crochet Accessories

Friendship Bracelets

EASY

The ultimate beginner's project and ideal for using up leftover scraps from other makes. You'll need a button to fasten them, so why not save one from a worn-out shirt, or seek out thrift stores and haberdasheries to find something unique to customise. Super fun, super easy and super quick. Swap with friends, send to a loved one, or make these bracelets in all the colours of the rainbow to wear with pride.

Measurements
One size
Approx. 21cm (8¼ in) long

What you will need
- Paintbox Yarns Cotton Aran
  100% cotton, 85m (93 yards) per 50g (1¾ oz)

Quantity:
Small amounts of the following colour (one colour per bracelet):
- **A** Lipstick Pink (652)
- **B** Blood Orange (620)
- **C** Buttercup Yellow (623)
- **D** Grass Green (630)
- **E** Marine Blue (634)
- **F** Sailor Blue (640)
- **G** Pale Lilac (646)
- 4mm (US G/6) crochet hook
- 12mm (½ in) button (one for each bracelet)
- Matching sewing thread and needle

Tension (gauge)
14 sts to 10cm (4 in) over dc using 4mm (US G/6) hook, or size required to achieve the correct tension (gauge).

Abbreviations
See page 61.

Special techniques
Working the knit stitch (also called waistcoat stitch, see page 87).
This stitch is just like a regular dc but instead of working the dc into the top two loops of the dc, it is worked through the two front vertical posts of the dc.

Notes
To adjust the length of the bracelet, add stitches on to or take stitches away from the first row of chain stitches.

To make

Using 4mm (US G/6) hook and chosen colour, ch31.
Row 1 (RS): Work 1dc in 2nd ch from hook, work 1dc in every ch to end of row, turn. *30dc.*
Row 2: Ch1, work 1 knit st (see Notes on page 85) in every dc to end of row, ch5 for button loop, sl st in 1st dc of Row 1.
Cut yarn and draw end through final dc to fasten off.

To finish

Weave in any yarn ends.
Gently steam bracelet to lie flat.
Sew a button onto the opposite end from the button loop.

Masterclass

Working the knit stitch

By working the double crochet stitch in a slightly different way it's possible to create a fabric made up of lots of Vs in vertical columns that actually resembles knitted stocking (stockinette) stitch. Insert the hook in between the "legs" of the V of the dc on the row below. When working this stitch, it is worth going up a hook size than recommended on the yarn label as you need the stitches to be loose enough to be able to insert the hook into the Vs.

One Insert the hook into the centre of the double crochet stitch in the row below, between the two vertical strands of yarn that for the "legs" of the V. Flip the work so you can see the wrong side of the fabric. The hook must emerge between the two vertical strands at the back of the double crochet stitch and under the horizontal strand.

Two Finish the double crochet stitch as usual by working yarn round hook and drawing a loop through. Work yarn round hook and draw it through both loops on the hook. You have completed one knit stitch.

Three Repeat these steps to work a knit stitch in each double crochet on the previous row or round. Continue working in this way to create a fabric that resembles knitted stocking stitch.

EASY

Tote Bag

If "reduce, reuse, and recycle" is your mantra, this crocheted tote is just your bag. Replace single-use plastic with this shopper, ideal for carrying your everyday essentials; eco-friendly, handmade, and chic. Made by working in the round to be seam free, and with a heart motif to show how much you care. Why not make it as a gift, or size it up by using fatter yarn and a larger hook to create a beach bag.

Measurements
Approx. 30cm (12 in) wide x 35cm (13¾ in) long, excluding handles
Approx. 55cm (21¾ in) long, with handles

What you will need
- Rico Essentials Cotton DK
  100% cotton, 120m (131 yards) per 50g (1¾ oz)

Quantity:
- 3 x 50g (1¾ oz) balls in Alga (73)
- 3mm (US C/2 or D/3) crochet hook
- 3.5mm (US E/4) crochet hook
- Yarn needle

Tension (gauge)
Approx. 8 blocks and 9 rounds to 10cm (4 in) over patt using 3.5mm (US E/4) hook, or size required to achieve the correct tension (gauge).

Abbreviations
See page 61.

Special techniques
Working filet crochet (see pages 92–93).

Notes
This design uses a technique called filet crochet to create a heart motif. Filet crochet is worked by forming an open mesh for the background (called open squares) and filling in the open squares to form the motif pattern (called closed squares).
An open square is made over 3 stitches, working [1tr, ch2, miss ch2-sp].
A closed square is made over 3 stitches, working [1tr in next tr and 2tr in ch2-sp] to fill the square.
A chart is provided for the heart motif, which is worked in closed squares. The motif is placed on the first half (front) of the bag. When working from the chart, read each round from right to left, starting in the bottom righthand corner.

Crochet Accessories

To make

Main bag

Using 3.5mm (US E/4) hook, ch144 and join with a sl st to 1st ch to form a large ring, making sure the chain is not twisted.
Next round (RS): Ch5 (counts as 1tr and ch2-sp), miss 2 ch, [1tr in next ch, ch2, miss 2 ch] to end of round, sl st to 3rd ch of beg ch5. *48 open squares.*
Next round (RS): Ch5 (counts as 1tr and ch2-sp), miss ch2-sp, [1tr in next tr, ch2, miss ch2-sp] to end of round, sl st to 3rd ch of beg ch5.
Rep last round 10 times more.
Start working from Round 1 of chart as follows:
Round 1: Starting with ch5 as before, work 12 open squares in total, 1 closed square, then [1tr in next tr, ch2, miss ch2-sp] to end of round and sl st to 3rd ch of beg ch5.
Cont in this way, following Rounds 2 to 15 of chart, plus 5 open rounds.
Change to 3mm (US C/2 or D/3) hook.
Next round: Ch1 (does not count as a st throughout), 1dc into each tr and 2dc in each ch2-sp to end of round, sl st to beg ch1. *144 sts.*
Next round: Ch1, 1dc in each dc to end of round, sl st to beg ch1.
Repeat last round twice more.
Do not fasten off; continue with handles.

Handles (make 2)

Round 1: Ch1, 1dc in next 21 dc, ch90 to make first handle, miss next 30dc, 1dc in next 42dc, ch90 to make second handle, miss next 30dc, 1dc in each st to end of round, sl st to beg ch1. *324 sts.*
Round 2: Ch1, 1dc in each dc and ch to end of round, sl st to beg ch1.
Round 3: Ch1, 1dc in each dc to end of round, sl st to beg ch1.
Repeat last round 3 times more.
Cut yarn and draw end through final stitch to fasten off.

To finish

Weave in any yarn ends.
Join the bottom seam on the inside of the bag by hand-sewing with whip stitch or using a crochet slip stitch, making sure the heart motif sits centrally on the front side.

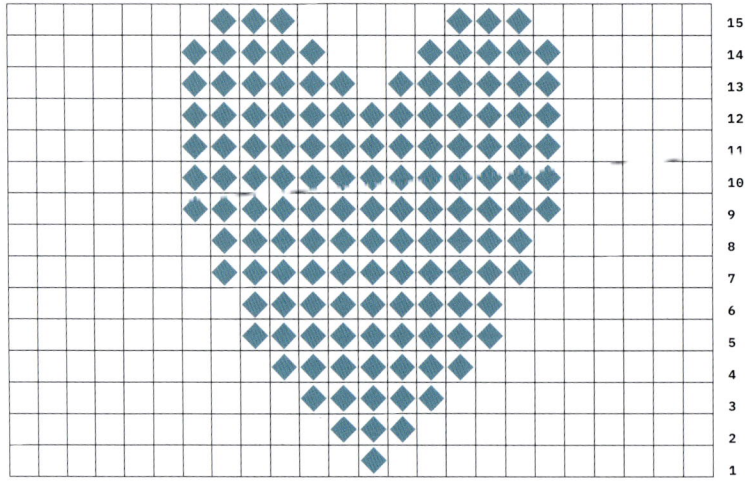

Key: □ open square
      ◆ closed square

Masterclass

Working filet crochet

Crochet is such a versatile yarncraft: it can create an incredibly dense and sturdy fabric where the stitches are tightly packed, or it can be used to create a fluid, lacy fabric through openwork techniques where the open spaces play just as an important role as the chains that separate them.

Filet crochet is the easiest of all the openwork techniques. Once you learn how to work the simple structure of the open squares or mesh and the closed squares or blocks, all you need to do is follow a simple chart to form motifs, such as the heart on the tote bag, or any other geometric pattern.

Reading filet crochet charts

Filet crochet charts are the simplest of all. The chart on page 90 shows the heart motif, indicating which squares of the filet mesh need to be filled in as solid blocks in order to form the heart shape. Each square on the chart represents either a filet space or a filet block. The heart motif is a symmetrical design, but lefthanded crocheters do need to work from filet crochet charts and instructions in a mirror image.

Start working from the filet crochet chart as instructed in the pattern to place the motif in the correct position. Working the chart from the bottom upwards, make the blocks and spaces on the chart. Because this tote bag is made in the round, all the rows are read from right to left. However, if you are working in rows then read the first row and all following odd-numbered rows from right to left, and then even-numbered rows from left to right.

Making a basic filet open square

The basic open filet square is made up of alternating trebles and 2 chains to form an open grid or mesh. The trebles sit on top of each other to stack vertically, while the chains sit horizontally, except the turning chains that link the side edges.

Making basic filet closed square

The pattern motifs of filet crochet are created by filling in some of the mesh squares and leaving others empty. In other words, the designs are built up with solid squares and square holes. Having learned how to work the open filet mesh, understanding how to fill them in to form solid blocks is easy. Rather than making 2 chains between each treble, work 2 trebles instead to fill in a solid block. The rules are very simple: working chains forms an empty square, working trebles fills in the square.

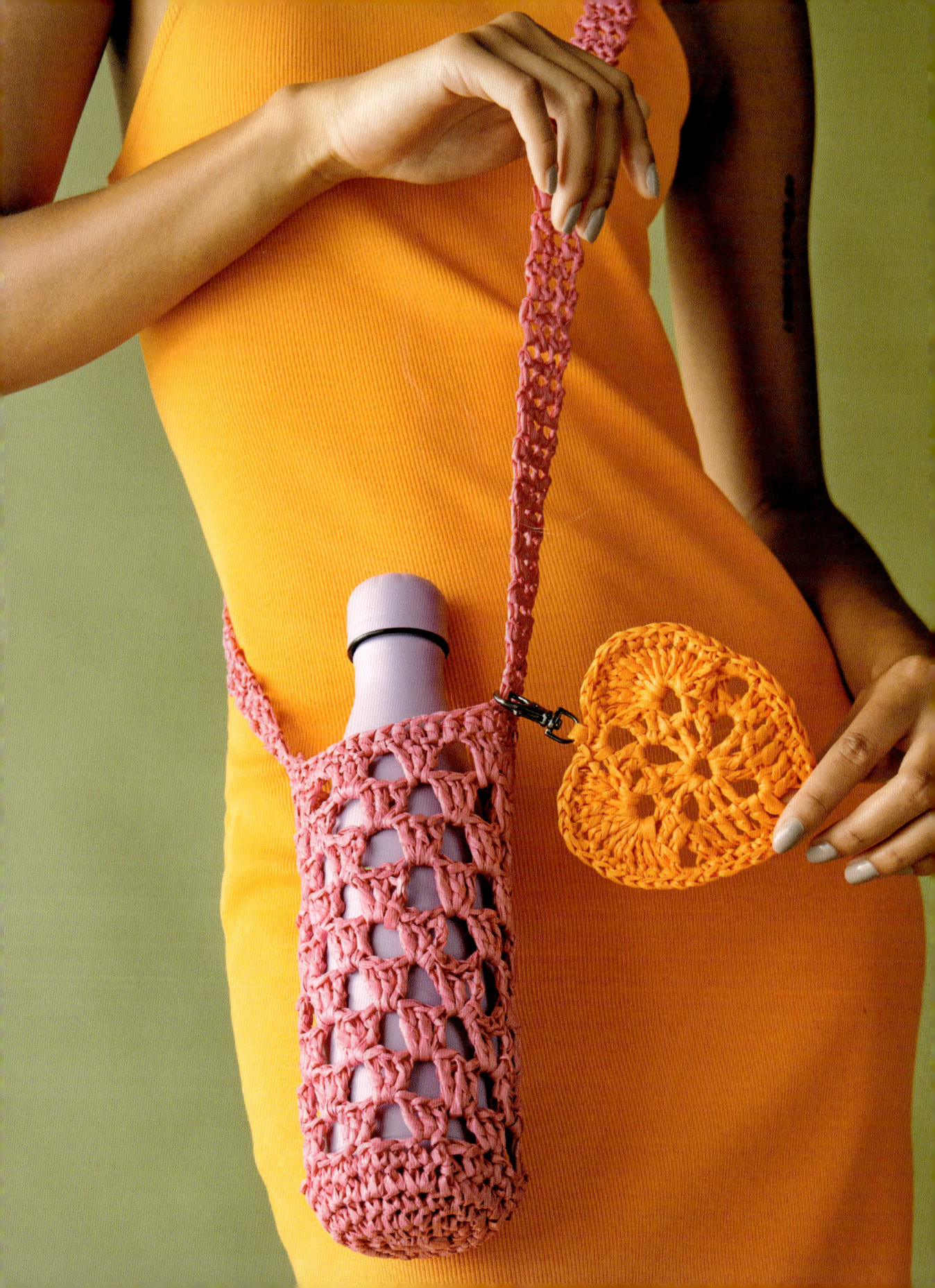

Bottle Carrier

EASY

Keeping hydrated has never looked so cool. Made in paper raffia for durability and style, this is a highly practical project to carry your water bottle around a festival, to the beach, or just on the daily commute. I like to make them to transport a bottle to a dinner party, and then the bottle carrier becomes a gift for the host too. Personalise with a keyring in a coordinating colour like I have, using the heart keyring from pages 108–111.

Tension (gauge)
4 blocks of 3tr and 1ch and 6 rows to 10cm (4 in) over patt using 4.5mm (US 7) hook, or size required to achieve the correct tension (gauge).

Abbreviations
See page 61.

Notes
Move the stitch marker onto the last stitch of every round as you work.

Measurements
One size
Approx. 10cm (4 in) in diameter and 15cm (6 in) high, excluding strap

What you will need
- Wool and the Gang RaRa Raffia 100% paper, 250m (273 yards) per 100g (3½ oz)

Quantity:
- 1 x 100g (3½ oz) ball in Vitamin C (or Hot Pink)
- 4.5mm (US 7) crochet hook
- Stitch marker
- Yarn needle

To make

Base ring: Using 4.5mm (US 7) hook, ch6 and join with a sl st in 1st ch to form a ring.
Round 1 (RS): Ch1 (does not count as a st), 8dc into ring, placing marker on last st. *8dc.*
Round 2: 2dc in each dc to end of round. *16dc.*
Round 3: *1dc in next dc, 2dc in next dc, rep from * to end of round. *24dc.*
Round 4: 1dc in each dc to end of round.
Round 5: *1dc in next dc, 2dc in next dc, rep from * to end of round. *36dc.*
Round 6: 1dc in each dc to end of round, join with a sl st to 1st dc. Remove marker.
Round 7: Ch3 (counts as 1st tr), 2 tr in same place as beg ch3, ch1, (miss 3 dc, 3tr in next dc, ch1) 8 times, miss 3 dc, sl st to 3rd ch of beg ch3.
Round 8: Sl st in next 2tr, sl st in ch1-sp, 3ch (counts as 1st tr), 2tr into same ch1-sp, ch1, *3tr in next ch1-sp, ch1, rep from * to end of round, sl st to 3rd ch of beg ch3. Repeat last round 7 times more.
Round 16: Ch2 (counts as 1st htr), 1htr in next 2 tr, 1htr in next ch1-sp, *1htr in next 3 tr, 1htr in next ch1-sp, rep from * to end of round, sl st to 2nd ch of beg ch2, sl st in next htr.

Make first handle

Next row: Ch1 (does not count as a st), 1dc in next 3 htr, turn. *3htr.*
Next row: Ch1, 1dc in next 3dc, turn. *3dc.*
Repeat last row until strap meas 65cm (25½ in). Fasten off, leaving a long yarn end.

Make second handle

Miss next 15 htr to left of first handle. Rejoin yarn with sl st to next htr and work as follows:
Next row: Ch1, 1dc in next 3 htr, turn. *3htr.*
Next row: Ch1, 1dc in next 3 dc, turn. *3dc.*
Repeat last row until strap meas 65cm (25½ in). Fasten off, leaving a long yarn end.

To finish

Join both handles, making sure they are not twisted. Fasten off very securely. Weave in any yarn ends. Customise as preferred.

EASY

Bucket Hat

It only takes a couple of hours of chilled mindful crocheting to make this '90s-style bucket hat – the ultimate in summer festival chic. Using a combination of crochet techniques and motifs this is a quick accessory to crochet for yourself – I bet pretty soon all your friends will want to be in the gang too! Pair your bucket hat with the bottle carrier on pages 94–97 and you're ready for the main stage.

Measurements
One size
To fit approx. circumference of head 60cm (23¾ in)
A larger hat can be made using a 5.5mm (US I/9) crochet hook throughout

What you will need
- Wool and the Gang RaRa Raffia 100% paper, 250m (273 yards) per 100g (3½ oz)

Quantity:

Colourway 1
- **A** 1 x 100g (3½ oz) ball in Vitamin C
- **B** 1 x 100g (3½ oz) ball in Coal Black

Colourway 2
- **A** 1 x 100g (3½ oz) ball in Hot Pink
- **B** 1 x 100g (3½ oz) ball in Coal Black

- 5mm (US H/8) crochet hook
- Yarn needle

Tension (gauge)
12sts and 10 rows to 10cm (4 in) over htr using 5mm (US H/8) hook, or size required to achieve the correct tension (gauge).

Abbreviations
See page 61.

Note
Ch2 at the start of each round counts as the 1st htr.

To make

Top of hat

Using 5mm (US H/8) hook and **A**, ch4 and join with a sl st to 1st ch to form a ring.
Round 1 (RS): Ch2 (counts as 1st htr throughout), 13htr into ring, join with a sl st 2nd ch of beg ch2. *14 sts.*
Round 2: Ch2, 2htr in next st, (1htr in next st, 2htr in next st) 6 times, sl st to 2nd ch of beg ch2. *21 sts.*
Round 3: Ch2, 1htr in next st, 2htr in next st, (1htr in next 2 sts, 2htr in next st) 6 times, sl st to 2nd ch of beg ch2. *28 sts.*
Round 4: Ch2, 1htr in next 2 sts, 2htr in next st, (1htr in next 3 sts, 2htr in next st) 6 times, sl st to 2nd ch of beg ch2. *35 sts.*
Round 5: Ch2, 1htr in next 3 sts, 2htr in next st, (1htr in next 4 sts, 2htr in next st) 6 times, sl st to 2nd ch of beg ch2. *42 sts.*
Round 6: Ch2, 1htr in next 4 sts, 2htr in next st, (1htr in next 5 sts, 2htr in next st) 6 times, sl st to 2nd ch of beg ch2. *49 sts.*
Round 7: Ch2, 1htr in next 5 sts, 2htr in next st, (1htr in next 6 sts, 2htr in next st) 6 times, sl st to 2nd ch of ch2. *56 sts.*
Round 8: Ch2, 1htr in next 6 sts, 2 htr in next st, (1htr in next 7 sts, 2htr in next st) 6 times, sl st to 2nd ch of beg ch2. *63 sts.*
Fasten off.

Motifs (make 7)

Using 5mm (US H/8) hook and **B** (for Colourway 1) or continuing in **A** (for Colourway 2), ch4 and join with a sl st in 1st ch to form a ring.
Round 1 (RS): Ch5 (counts as 1tr and 2ch), (3tr, 2ch) 3 times into ring, 2tr into ring, join with a sl st to 3rd ch of beg ch5.
4 groups of 3tr and 4 ch2-sp.
Fasten off.
Join **A** with a sl st to any ch2 corner space and work as follows:
Round 2: Ch5 (counts as 1tr and 2ch), 3tr in same corner sp, *1ch, (3tr, 2ch, 3tr) in next 2ch corner sp, rep from * twice more, ch1, 2tr in same sp as ch5 at beg of round, sl st to 3rd ch of beg ch5.
8 groups of 3 tr and 4 ch2-sp.
Fasten off leaving a long end of approx. 50cm (20 in) for sewing motifs together.

When all 7 motifs are complete, join motifs together using yarn ends to whip stitch through adjoining stitches to make a long strip. Join ends of long strip to make a circular band.
Sew the edge of top of hat to one edge of this circular band.

Brim

With RS of hat facing, rejoin **A** with a sl st to corner of any one of the motifs and work as follows:
Next round: Ch2 (counts as 1htr throughout), work 8htr across first motif, then work 9htr across each of rem six motifs, join with a sl st to 2nd ch of beg ch2. *63 sts.*
Next round: Ch2, *1htr in next st, 2htr in next st. rep from * to end of round, sl st to 2nd ch of beg ch2. *94 sts.*
Next round: Ch2, *1htr in next st, rep from * to end of round, sl st to 2nd ch of beg ch2.
Repeat last round twice more, changing to **B** on last yrh of last st, ready to work spiky edging as follows:
Next round: Ch2, *1htr in each of next 2 sts, miss next st and work a htr into row below this st as follows: yrh, insert hook through space in row below, yrh and draw through, yrh and draw through 3 loops on hook, rep from * to end of round.
Fasten off.

To finish

Weave in any yarn ends.

EASY

Cosy Slippers

The first thing I do when I get home is kick off my shoes and get cosy in my slippers. This boot-style version is stylish and soft, crocheted in super chunky 100% merino wool, to keep toes and ankles toasty. Quick to make for you and for the whole family, with a junior size, then get creative and customise with stripes and pompoms.

Measurements

Adult size	M	L	
Foot length	24.5	27.5	cm
	9½	11	in

Junior size	XS	S	
Foot length	18.5	21.5	cm
	7¼	8½	in

What you will need
- Wool Couture Cheeky Chunky 100% merino wool, 65m (71 yards) per 100g (3½ oz)

ADULT SIZE Quantity:
- **A** 3 x 100g (3½ oz) balls in Aquamarine
- **B** 1 x 100g (3½ oz) ball in Black
- **C** 1 x 100g (3½ oz) ball in Aqua
- **D** 1 x 100g (3½ oz) ball in Mustard
- **E** 1 x 100g (3½ oz) ball in Raspberry
- **F** 1 x 100g (3½ oz) ball in Natural Cream

JUNIOR SIZE Quantity:
- 2 x 100g (3½ oz) balls in Raspberry
- Scraps in random colours, for pompoms
- 6mm (US J/10) crochet hook
- 7mm (US K/10½ or US L/11) crochet hook
- Yarn needle

Tension (gauge)
10 sts and 12 rows to 10cm (4 in) over dc using 7mm (US K/10½ or US L/11) hook, or size required to achieve the correct tension (gauge).

Abbreviations
See page 61.
dc2tog (insert hook in next st, yrh and draw loop through) twice, yrh and draw through all 3 loops on hook. One stitch decreased.

Special techniques
Changing colour at the end of a row (see page 107).
Making pompoms (see page 75).

Note
The slippers are made in two separate pieces – the upper and the sole.

To make adult size

Slipper upper (make 2)

Leg
Working in rounds, using 7mm (US K/10½ or US L/11) hook and **A**, ch30[33] and join with a sl st to form a ring (making sure chain is not twisted when chain is joined).
Round 1 (RS): Ch1, 1dc in same place as sl st, 1dc in each ch to end of round, join with a sl st to 1st dc. *30[33] sts.*
Round 2: Ch1, 1dc in same place as sl st, 1dc in each st to end of round, join with a sl st to 1st dc.
Repeat last round 6 times more.
Do not fasten off; continue with heel.

Heel
Work in rows as follows:
Next row: Ch1, 1dc in same place as sl st, 1dc in each st to end of round, turn. *30[33] sts.*
Next row: Ch1, 1dc in each st to end of row, turn. *30[33] sts.*
Next row (dec): Ch1, dc2tog, 1dc in each st to last 2 sts, dc2tog, turn. *29[31] sts.*
Next row: Ch1, 1dc in each st to end of row, turn.
Repeat last row 1[2] times more.
Do not fasten off; continue with instep.

Instep
Work in rounds as follows:
Next round: Ch1, 2dc in 1st dc, 1dc in each st to last dc, 2dc in last dc, then work 11[13]dc across instep row ends, join with a sl st to 1st dc.
Next round: Ch1, 1dc in same place as sl st, 1dc in each st to end of round, change to **B** and join with a sl st to 1st dc, turn.
Do not fasten off; continue with top of foot.

Top of foot
Work in rows, changing colours where indicated.
Next row: Using **B**, ch1, 1dc in next 14[16] sts, changing to **C** on last st, turn. *14[16] sts.*
Size L only
Next row: Using **C**, ch1, 1dc in next 16 sts, turn. *16 sts.*
Both sizes
Next row: Using **C**, ch1, 1dc in next 14[16] sts, changing to **D** on last st, turn. *14[16] sts.*
Next row: Using **D**, ch1, 1dc in next 14[16] sts, turn.
Next row: Using **D**, ch1, 1dc in next 14[16] sts, changing to **E** on last st, turn.
Size L only
Next row: Using **E**, ch1, 1dc in next 16 sts, turn. *16 sts.*
Both sizes
Next row (dec): Using **E**, ch1, 1dc in each st to last 2 sts, dc2tog, changing to **F** on last st, turn. *13[15] sts.*
Next row (dec): Using **F**, ch1, 1dc in each st to last 2 sts, dc2tog, turn. *12[14] sts.*
Next row: Using **F**, ch1, 1dc in each st to end of row, changing to **B** on last st, turn.
Next row: Using **B**, ch1, 1dc in each st to end of row, turn.
Next row (dec): ch1, 1dc in each dc to last 2 sts, dc2tog, changing to **A** on last st, turn. *11[13] sts.*
Next row (dec): Using **A**, ch1, 1dc in each st to last 2 sts, dc2tog, turn. *10[12] sts.*
Next row (dec): Using **A**, ch1, 1dc in each st to last 2 sts, dc2tog, changing to **C** on last st. *9[11] sts.*
Next row (dec): Using **C**, ch1, 1dc in each st to last 2 sts, dc2tog, turn. *8[10] sts.*
Fasten off.

Sole (make 2)

Using 7mm (US K/10½ or US L/11) hook and **A**, ch6[7] and work in rows as follows:
Row 1: 1dc in 2nd ch from hook, 1dc in each ch to end, turn. *5[6] sts.*
Row 2: Ch1, 1dc in each st to end of row, turn.
Row 3 (inc): Ch1, 2dc in 1st st, 1dc in each st to last st, 2dc in next st, turn. *7[8] sts.*
Row 4: Ch1, 1dc in each st to end of row, turn.
Repeat last row until sole meas 13[15]cm (5¼[6] in).
Next row (inc): Ch1, 2dc in 1st st, 1dc in each st to last st, 2dc in last st, turn. *9[10] sts.*
Next row: Ch1, 1dc in each st to end of row, turn.

Repeat last row until sole meas 22.5[25.5]cm (9[10] in).
Next row (dec): Ch1, dc2tog, 1dc in each st to last 2 sts, dc2tog, turn. *7[8] sts*.
Next row (dec): Ch1, dc2tog, 1dc in each st to last 2 sts, dc2tog, turn. *5[6] sts*.
Fasten off.

To finish

See instructions below.

To make junior size

Slipper upper (make 2)

Leg
Working in rounds, using 7mm (US K/10½ or US L/11) hook, ch23[27] and join with a sl st to form a ring (making sure chain is not twisted when chain is joined).
Round 1 (RS): Ch1, 1dc in same place as sl st, 1dc in each ch to end of round, join with a sl st to 1st dc. *23[27] sts*.
Round 2: Ch1, 1dc in same place as sl st, 1dc in each st to end of round, join with a sl st to 1st dc.
Repeat last round 3[4] times more.
Do not fasten off; continue with heel.

Heel
Work in rows as follows:
Next row: Ch1, 1dc in same place as sl st, 1dc in each st to end of round, turn. *23[27] sts*.
Next row (dec): Ch1, dc2tog, 1dc in each st to last 2 sts, dc2tog, turn. *21[25] sts*.
Next row: Ch1, 1dc in each st to end of row, turn.
Do not fasten off; continue with instep.

Instep
Work in rounds as follows:
Next round: Ch1, 1dc in each st to end of previous row, then work 8[10]dc across instep row ends, join with a sl st to 1st dc.
Next round: Ch1, 1dc in same place as sl st, 1dc in each st to end of round, join with a sl st to 1st dc, turn.

Do not fasten off; continue with top of foot.
Top of foot
Work in rows.
Next row: Ch1, 1dc in next 9[11] sts, turn. *9[11] sts*.
Repeat last row 4[5] times more.
Next row (dec): Ch1, 1dc in each st to last 2 sts, dc2tog, turn. *8[10] sts*.
Repeat last row 3 times more. *5[7] sts*.
Fasten off.

Sole (make 2)

Using 7mm (US K/10½ or US L/11) hook, ch4 and work in rows as follows:
Row 1: 1dc in 2nd ch from hook, 1dc in next 2 ch, turn. *3[4] sts*.
Row 2: Ch1, 1dc in each st to end of row, turn.
Row 3 (inc): Ch1, 2dc in 1st st, 1dc in next st, 2dc in next st, turn. *5[6] sts*.
Row 4: Ch1, 1dc in each st to end of row, turn.
Repeat last row until sole meas 9.5[11.5]cm (3¾[4½] in).
Next row (inc): Ch1, 2dc in 1st st, 1dc in each st to last st, 2dc in last st, turn. *7[8] sts*.
Next row: Ch1, 1dc in each st to end of row, turn.
Repeat last row until sole meas 15.5[18.5]cm (6[7¼] in).
Next row (dec): Ch1, dc2tog, 1dc in each st to last 2 sts, dc2tog, turn. *5[6] sts*.
Next row (dec): Ch1, dc2tog, 1dc in next st, dc2tog, turn. *3[4] sts*.
Fasten off.

To finish

Pin sole to upper, easing to fit. Using 6mm (US J/10) hook, join yarn with a sl st to centre of heel. Inserting hook through both layers, ch1 and work dc all around. Join with a sl st to 1st dc. Fasten off. Weave in any yarn ends.

Adding pompoms (make 2)
Using scraps of different yarns, make two pompoms (see page 75). Use the long yarn ends to secure the pompoms, then sew them securely to each slipper toe.

Masterclass

Changing colour at the end of a row

Swapping colours between rows is a useful technique to learn, as it opens the door to all kinds of striped and colour block crochet projects. You can also use this technique to add a new ball of the same colour yarn when you run out.

One — Work all the way along the row, stopping when there is just one stitch left to go. Crochet this stitch as usual, until you get to the final stage when you are about to pull the yarn through the last two loops on the hook. Let the working yarn drop down and hold the new yarn across your hook, leaving a 20cm (6 inch) yarn tail.

Two — Wrap the new colour yarn around your hook anti-clockwise and draw it through the final two loops to complete the last stitch of the row.

Three — Turn the work and make the required number of turning chains from the new yarn. Continue stitching as usual along the row.

Four — Tie the yarn tails together with a knot to stop the edges unravelling. You can weave them in and trim the ends now, or wait until your piece is finished.

Heart Keyring

When you need a quick crafty fix, this keyring is great for working up easily on the go. Use up leftover yarn from larger projects and combine motifs, letters, and tassels to make unique keyrings. Clip on your handbag, lunchbox, bottle carrier, suitcase, gift... Let your imagination go wild.

Measurements
Heart approx. 11cm (4¼ in) long
Letter approx. 14cm (5½ in) long
Tassel approx. 14cm (5½ in) long

What you will need
- Wool and the Gang RaRa Raffia 100% paper, 250m (273 yards) per 100g (3½ oz)

Quantity:
- 1 x 100g (3½ oz) ball in Vitamin C
- 4.5mm (US 7) crochet hook
- Yarn needle
- Lobster clasp keyring

Tension (gauge)
An exact tension (gauge) is not critical for this project.

Abbreviations
See page 61.

Special techniques
Working shells (see page 111).

To make

Heart

Using 4.5mm (US 7) hook, ch4 and join with a sl st in 1st ch to form a ring.
Round 1 (RS): Ch3 (counts as 1tr), 2tr into ring, (ch2, 3tr into ring) 3 times, ch2, join with a sl st to 3rd ch of beg ch3. *4 groups of 3tr and 4 ch2-sp.*
Round 2: Ch3 (counts as 1tr), 1tr in sp between beg ch3 and next tr, 1tr in sp between next 2 tr, (2tr, ch2, 2tr) in corner sp, *(1tr in sp between next 2tr) twice, (2tr, ch2, 2tr) in corner sp, rep from * once more, (1tr in sp between next 2tr) twice, (2tr, ch2, 1tr) in corner sp, sl st to 3rd ch of beg ch3. *6tr along each side and 4 ch2-sp.*
Fasten off.

Top right section of heart

With RS facing, rejoin yarn between 3rd and 4th tr of one side and work as follows:
Next round (part round): Ch3 (counts as 1tr), 5tr in same sp at base of beg ch3, 6dtr in same sp. *12 sts.* Fasten off.

Top left section of heart

With RS facing, rejoin yarn between 3rd and 4th tr of next side and work as follows:
Next round (part round): Ch4 (counts as 1dtr), 5dtr in same sp at base of beg ch4, 6tr in same sp. *12 sts.* Fasten off.

With RS facing, rejoin yarn with a sl st to ch2-sp at base of heart and work as follows:
Final round: Ch1, 2dc in same sp, 1dc in next 6 tr, 2dc in next ch2-sp, now work into sts from part rounds as follows: 1dc in 6 tr and 6 dtr of right section of heart, 3dc in next ch2-sp, 1dc in next 6 dtr and 6 tr of left section of heart, 2dc in next ch2-sp of Round 2, 1dc in next 6 tr, join with a sl st to beg ch1. *45 sts.*
Fasten off. Weave in any yarn ends.

Tassel

Cut 2 lengths, 50cm (20 in) long and set aside. Take a book or piece of cardboard approx. 18cm (7 in) long and wrap the leftover yarn approx. 30 times around the length (the more wraps the fuller the tassel will be). Cut the end of the yarn and slide the looped bundle off the book, holding it in the centre. Take one 50cm (20 in) length of yarn and fold in half. Thread the folded end through the looped bundle at one end. Tie it up by threading the two opposite ends through the folded yarn. Pull up tightly and knot securely. This will be the thread with which to fasten on to the keyring. Take the other 50cm (20 in) length and tie around the looped bundle 3cm (1¼ in) down from the hanging thread. Wind the ends around the bundle to secure, tuck in the ends, knot and trim off. Cut through the loops at the opposite end of the bundle, trim and gently shake out to create a tassel.

Letter

Follow instructions for chosen letter from pages 144–151, but using 4.5mm (US 7) hook.

To finish

To attach each element to the keyring clasp, use leftover yarn and thread through the top of each element, knotting securely. Weave in any yarn ends for a neat finish.

Masterclass

Working shells

The rounded upper corners of the heart motif are created by working lots of long stitches into a single space to create a fan-like effect. For a decorative finish, use the same technique to make a length of scalloped edge trim. This would also make a good border for a throw, worked directly into the edge of the crocheted fabric.

One Make a foundation chain, slightly longer than the length required. Add on the number of standing chains for the stitch you're using; these shells are made from double trebles (triple trebles), so there are four standing chain. Work the first double treble in the fifth chain from the hook.

Two Create the shell shape by making seven more double trebles into the same chain.

Three Skip the next four foundation chain and anchor the finished shell in place with a slip stitch in the fifth chain along. This gives you the same length as the standing chain and ensures the shell will lie flat.

Four Start the next shell with a double treble in the fifth chain along from the slip stitch and make seven more double trebles into the same chain. Anchor as before in the fifth chain along and repeat to the end of the foundation chain.

Crochet Garments

04

INTERMEDIATE

Polo Shirt

A crafty take on a classic "polo", this black and white shirt has a real beach-to-bar vibe. Designed in very simple pieces with little shaping, this garment is as easy to make as it is to wear. Crocheted in a cool, sustainable linen yarn with a good drape – it's the perfect shirt for every summer occasion.

Measurements
See chart below. The shirt is designed to be worn with approx. 4.5cm (1¾ in) to 19.5cm (7¾ in) ease.

What you will need
- Erika Knight Studio Linen
  85% recycled linen, 15% linen,
  120m (131 yards) per 50g (1¾ oz)

Quantity:
- **A** 7[8:9:10:11:12] x 50g (1¾ oz) balls in Kumo (411 – black)
- **B** 7[8:9:10:11:12] x 50g (1¾ oz) balls in Milk (400 – white)
- 3mm (US C/2 or D/3) crochet hook
- Stitch markers
- 5 buttons, 18mm (¾ in) in diameter
- Yarn needle

Tension (gauge)
22 sts and 11 rows to 10cm (4 in) over pattern using 3mm (US C/2 or D/3) hook, or size required to achieve the correct tension (gauge).

Abbreviations
See page 61.

Special technique
Using slip stitch to travel along a row (see page 121).

Notes
The back and fronts are crocheted from edge to edge.
Both fronts are the same because the wrong side and right side are nearly identical.
Change colour on last yoh of last st of row.
Ch3 at beg of row counts as 1tr.
Ch2 at beg of row counts as 1htr.

Adult size	XS	S/M	L/XL	XXL	XXXL	XXXXL	
Actual chest	103.5	111	122	136.5	147.5	154.5	cm
	40¾	43¾	48	53¾	58	61	in
Length	62	66	68	69.5	71	73	cm
	24½	26	26¾	27½	28	28¾	in
Sleeve length	18	18	19	19	20	20	cm
	7	7	7½	7½	8	8	in

Crochet Garments

To make

Back

Using 3mm (US C/2 or D/3) hook and **A**, ch140[148:152:156:160:164] and work as follows:
Row 1: 2tr in 4th ch from hook, ch1, *miss 3 ch, 3tr in next ch, ch1, rep from * to last 4 ch, miss 3 ch, 1tr in last ch, changing to **B** when finishing last st, turn. *34[36:37:38:39:40] x (3tr, ch1 clusters) and 1 tr; 137[145:149:153:157:161] sts.*
Row 2: Using **B**, ch3, 2tr in 1st ch1-sp, ch1, (3tr, 1ch) in every sp to end of row, 1tr in top of ch3, turn.
Row 3: Using **B**, ch3, 2tr in 1st ch1-sp, ch1, (3tr, ch1) in every sp to end of row, 1tr in top of ch3, turn.
Repeat last 2 rows 0[0:0:1:1:1] time more.
Row 4[4:4:6:6:6]: Using **B**, ch3, 2tr in 1st ch1-sp, ch1, (3tr, ch1) in every sp to end of row, 1tr in top of ch2, changing to **A**, turn.
Row 5[5:5:7:7:7]: Using **A**, ch3, 2tr in 1st ch1-sp, ch1, (3tr, ch1) in every sp to end of row, 1tr in top of ch3, changing to **B**, turn.
Row 6[6:6:8:8:8]: Using **B**, ch2, (1htr in 1st ch1-sp, 1htr into each of next 3tr) to last 3 sts, work 1htr into each of next 2tr and top of turning ch, changing to **A**, turn.
Row 7[7:7:9:9:9]: Using **A**, ch3, 2tr in 1st htr, ch1, (miss 3htr, 3tr in next htr, ch1) to last 2htr, miss these 2htr, 1tr in top of turning ch3, turn.
Row 8[8:8:10:10:10]: Using **A**, ch3, 2tr in 1st ch1-sp, ch1, (3tr, ch1) in every sp to end of row, 1tr in top of ch3, changing to **B** for sizes XS, S/M, L/XL and XXL, turn.

Sizes XXXL and XXXXL only

Repeat last row twice more, changing to **B** on last row, turn.

All sizes

Row 9[9:9:11:13:13]: Using **B**, ch3, 2tr in 1st ch1-sp, ch1, (3tr, ch1) in every sp of row, 1tr in top of ch3, turn.
Repeat last row 0[0:0:0:0:2] times more.
Row 10[10:10:12:14:16]: Using **B**, ch3, 2tr in 1st ch1-sp, ch1, (3tr, ch1) in every sp to end of row, 1tr in top of ch3, changing to **A**, turn.
Row 11[11:11:13:15:17]: Using **A**, ch3, 2tr in 1st ch1-sp, ch1, (3tr, ch1) in every sp to end of row, 1tr in top of ch3, turn.
Row 12[12:12:14:16:18]: Using **A**, ch3, 2tr in 1st ch1-sp, ch1, (3tr, ch1) in every sp to end of row, 1tr in top of ch3, turn.
Row 13[13:13:15:17:19]: Using **A**, ch3, 2tr in 1st ch1-sp, ch1, (3tr, ch1) in every sp to end of row, 1tr in top of ch3, turn.
Row 14[14:14:16:18:20]: Using **A**, ch3, 2tr in 1st ch1-sp, ch1, (3tr, ch1) in every sp to end of row, 1tr in top of ch3, turn.
Repeat last row 0[1:2:3:3:3] time(s) more, changing to **B** on last row, turn.
Row 15[16:17:20:22:24]: Using **B**, ch3, 2tr in 1st ch1-sp, ch1, (3tr, ch1) in every sp to end of row, 1tr in top of ch3, turn.
Row 16[17:18:21:23:25]: Using **B**, ch3, 2tr in 1st ch1-sp, ch1, (3tr, ch1) in every sp to end of row, 1tr in top of ch3, turn.
Row 17[18:19:22:24:26]: Using **B**, ch3, 2tr in 1st ch1-sp, ch1, (3tr, ch1) in every sp to end of row, 1tr in top of ch3, turn.
Row 18[19:20:23:25:27]: Using **B**, ch3, 2tr in 1st ch1-sp, ch1, (3tr, ch1) in every sp to end of row, 1tr in top of ch3, turn.
Repeat last row 0[1:2:3:3:3] time(s) more, changing to **A** on last row, turn.
Row 19[21:23:27:29:31]: Using **A**, ch3, 2tr in 1st ch1-sp, ch1, (3tr, ch1) in every sp to end of row, 1tr in top of ch3, changing to **B**, turn.
Row 20[22:24:28:30:32]: Using **B**, ch2, (1htr in next ch1-sp, 1htr into each of next 3 tr) to last 3 sts, work 1htr into each of next 2 tr and top of turning ch, changing to **A**, turn.
Place marker to show end of shoulder.**

Back neck

Row 21[23:25:29:31:33]: Using **A**, ch3, 2tr in 1st htr, ch1, (miss 3 htr, 3tr in next htr, ch1) to last 3 sts, miss 2htr, 1tr in top of turning ch.
Row 22[24:26:30:32:34]: Using **A**, ch3, 2tr in 1st ch1-sp, ch1, (3tr, ch1) in every sp to end of row, 1tr in top of ch3, turn.
Row 23[25:27:31:33:35]: Using **A**, ch3, 2tr in 1st ch1-sp, ch1, (3tr, ch1) in every sp to end of row, 1tr in top of ch3, turn.

Row 24[26:28:32:34:36]: Using **A**, ch3, 2tr in 1st ch1-sp ch, (3tr, ch1) in every sp to end of row, 1tr in top of ch3, changing to **B**, turn.
Row 25[27:29:33:35:37]: Using **B**, ch3, 2tr in 1st ch1-sp, ch1, (3tr, ch1) in every sp to end of row, 1tr in top of ch3, turn. Repeat last row 0[0:0:0:2:2] times more, turn.
Row 26[28:30:34:38:40]: Using **B**, ch3, 2tr in 1st ch1-sp, ch1, (3tr, ch1) in every sp to end of row, 1tr in top of ch3, changing to **A**, turn.
Row 27[29:31:35:39:41]: Using **A**, ch2, (1htr in next ch1-sp, 1htr into each of next 3 tr) to last 3 sts, 1htr in each of next 2 tr and 1htr in top of turning ch, changing to **B**, turn.
Row 28[30:32:36:40:42]: Using **B**, ch2, (1htr in each htr) to end of row, 1htr in the top of turning ch, turn.
Row 29[31:33:37:41:43]: Using **B**, ch3, 2tr in 1st htr, ch1, (miss 3 htr, 3tr in next htr, ch1) to last 3 sts, miss 2 htr, 1tr in top of turning ch, turn
Repeat last row 0[0:2:2:0:0] times more.
Row 30[32:36:40:42:44]: Using **B**, ch2, (1htr in next ch1-sp, 1htr in each of next 3 tr) to last 3 sts, 1htr in each of next 2 htr and 1htr in top of turning ch, changing to **A** turn.
Row 31[33:37:41:43:45]: Using **A**, ch2, (1htr in each htr) to end of row, 1htr in top of turning ch, changing to **B**, turn.
Row 32[34:38:42:44:46]: Using **B**, ch3, 2tr in 1st htr, ch1, (miss 3 htr, 3tr in next htr, ch1) to last 3 sts, miss 2 htr, 1tr in top of turning ch, turn.
Repeat last row 0[0:0:0:2:2] times more.
Row 33[35:39:43:47:49]: Using **B**, ch3, 2tr in 1st ch1-sp, ch1, (3tr, ch1) in every sp to end of row, 1tr in top of ch3, changing to **A**, turn.
Row 34[36:40:44:48:50]: Using **A**, ch3, 2tr in 1st ch1-sp, ch1, (3tr, ch1) in every sp to end of row, 1tr in top of ch3, turn.
Row 35[37:41:45:49:51]: Using **A**, ch3, 2tr in 1st ch1-sp, ch1, (3tr, ch1) in every sp to end of row, 1tr in top of ch3, turn.
Row 36[38:42:46:50:52]: Using **A**, ch3, 2tr in 1st ch1-sp, ch1, (3tr, ch1) in every sp to end of row, 1tr in top of ch3, turn.
Row 37[39:43:47:51:53]: Using **A**, ch3, 2tr in 1st ch1-sp, ch1, (3tr, ch1) in every sp to end of row, 1tr in top of ch3, changing to **B**, turn. Place marker to show start of shoulder.

Shoulder
Row 38[40:44:48:52:54]: Using **B**, ch2, (1htr in next ch1-sp, 1htr in each of next 3 tr) to last 3 sts, 1htr in each of next 2 htr and 1htr in top of turning ch, changing to **A**, turn.
Row 39[41:45:49:53:55]: Using **A**, ch3, 2tr in 1st htr, ch1, (miss 3 htr, 3tr in next htr, ch1) to last 3 sts, miss 2 htr, 1tr in top of turning ch, changing to **B**, turn.
Row 40[42:46:50:54:56]: Using **B**, ch3, 2tr in 1st ch1-sp ch, (3tr, ch1) in every sp to end of row, 1tr in top of ch3, turn.
Row 41[43:47:51:55:57]: Using **B**, ch3, 2tr in 1st ch1-sp, ch1, (3tr, ch1) in every sp to end of row, 1tr in top of ch3, turn.
Row 42[44:48:52:56:58]: Using **B**, ch3, 2tr in 1st ch1-sp, ch1, (3tr, ch1) in every sp to end of row, 1tr in top of ch3, turn.
Row 43[45:49:53:57:59]: Using **B**, ch3, 2tr in 1st ch1-sp, ch1, (3tr, ch1) in every sp to end of row, 1tr in top of ch3, turn.
Repeat last row 0[1:2:3:3:3] time(s) more, changing to **A** on last row, turn.
Row 44[47:52:57:61:63]: Using **A**, ch3, 2tr in 1st ch1-sp, ch1, (3tr, ch1) in every sp to end of row, 1tr in top of ch3, turn.
Row 45[48:53:58:62:64]: Using **A**, ch3, 2tr in 1st ch1-sp, ch1, (3tr, ch1) in every sp to end of row, 1tr in top of ch3, turn.
Row 46[49:54:59:63:65]: Using **A**, ch3, 2tr in 1st ch1-sp, ch1, (3tr, ch1) in every sp to end of row, 1tr in top of ch3, turn.
Row 47[50:55:60:64:66]: Using **A**, ch3, 2tr in 1st ch1-sp, ch1, (3tr, ch1) in every sp to end of row, 1tr in top of ch3, turn.
Repeat last row 0[1:2:3:3:3] time(s) more, changing to **B** on last row, turn
Row 48[52:58:64:68:70]: Using **B**, ch3, 2tr in 1st ch1-sp, ch1, (3tr, ch1) in every sp to end of row, 1tr in top of ch3, turn.
Repeat last row 0[0:0:0:0:2] times more.

Row 49[53:59:65:69:73]: Using **B**, ch3, 2tr in 1st ch1-sp, ch1, (3tr, ch1) in every sp to end of row, 1tr in top of ch3, changing to **A**, turn.
Row 50[54:60:66:70:74]: Using **A**, ch3, 2tr in 1st ch1-sp, ch1, (3tr, ch1) in every sp to end of row, 1tr in top of ch3, turn.
Row 51[55:61:67:71:75]: Using **A**, ch3, 2tr in 1st ch1-sp, ch1, (3tr, ch1) in every sp to end of row, 1tr in top of ch3, changing to **B** for sizes XS, S/M, L/XL and XXL, turn.
Sizes XXXL and XXXXL only
Repeat last row twice more, changing to **B** on last row, turn.
All sizes
Row 52[56:62:68:74:78]: Using **B**, ch2, (1htr in next ch1-sp, 1htr in each of next 3 tr) to last 3 sts, 1htr in each of next 2 htr and 1htr in top of turning ch, changing to **A**, turn.
Row 53[57:63:69:75:79]: Using **A**, ch3, 2tr in 1st htr, ch1, (miss 3 htr, 3tr in next htr, ch1) to last 3 sts, miss 2 htr, 1tr in top of turning ch, changing to **B**, turn.
Row 54[58:64:70:76:80]: Using **B**, ch3, 2tr in 1st ch1-sp, ch1, (3tr, ch1) in every sp to end of row, 1tr in top of ch3, turn.
Row 55[59:65:71:77:81]: Using **B**, ch3, 2tr in 1st ch1-sp, ch1, (3tr, ch1) in every sp to end of row, 1tr in top of ch3, turn.
Repeat last row 0[0:0:2:2:2] times more.
Row 56[60:66:74:80:84]: Using **B**, ch3, 2tr in 1st ch1-sp, ch1, (3tr, ch1) in every sp to end of row, 1tr in top of ch3, changing to **A**, turn.
Row 57[61:67:75:81:85]: Using **A**, ch3, 2tr in 1st ch1-sp, ch1, (3tr, ch1) in every sp to end of row, 1tr in top of ch3.
Fasten off.

Fronts (make two the same)

Work as given for back to ** but do not change to **A** on last st. *20[22:24:28:30:32] rows worked.*

Shape neck

Using **B**, sl st in 1st 5htr, then change to **A**.
Row 21[23:25:29:31:33]: Using **A**, ch3, 2tr in the same st, ch1, (miss 3 htr, 3tr in next htr, ch1) to last 3 sts, miss 2 htr, 1tr in turning ch, turn.
Row 22[24:26:30:32:34]: Using **A**, ch3, 2tr in 1st ch1-sp, ch1, (3tr, ch1) in every sp until 2 blocks from the end, 1tr in last ch-sp, turn.
Row 23[25:27:31:33:35]: Using **A**, ch3, 2tr in 1st ch1-sp, ch1, (3tr, ch1) in every sp to end of row, 1tr in top of ch3, turn.
Row 24[26:28:32:34:36]: Using **A**, ch3, 2tr in 1st ch1-sp, ch1, (3tr, ch1) in every sp until 2 blocks from the end, 1tr in top of ch3, changing to **B**, turn.
Row 25[27:29:33:35:37]: Using **B**, ch3, 2tr in 1st ch1-sp, ch1, (3tr, ch1) in every sp to end of row, 1tr in top of ch3, turn.
31[33:34:35:36:37] x [3tr, ch1 clusters] and 2tr.
Row 26[28:30:34:36:38]: Using **B**, ch3, 2tr in 1st ch1-sp, ch1, (3tr, ch1) in every sp to end of row, 1tr in top of ch3, changing to **A** for sizes XS, S/M, L/XL and XXL, turn.
Sizes XXXL and XXXXL only
Repeat last row twice more, changing to **A** on last row, turn.
All sizes
Row 27[29:31:35:39:41]: Using **A**, ch2, (1htr in 1st ch1-sp, 1htr into each of next 3 tr) to last 3 sts, work 1htr into each of next 2 tr and 1htr in top of turning ch, changing to **B**, turn.
Row 28[30:32:36:40:42]: Using **B**, ch2, (1htr in each htr) to end of row, 1htr in top of turning ch, turn.
Row 29[31:33:37:41:43]: Using **B**, ch3, 2tr in 1st htr, ch1, (miss 3 htr, 3tr in next htr, ch1) to last 3 sts, miss 2 htr, 1tr in top of turning ch, turn.
Repeat last row 0[0:2:2:0:0] times more.
Row 30[32:36:40:42:44]: Using **B**, ch2, (1htr in 1st ch1-sp, 1htr into each of next 3tr) to last 3 sts, work 1htr into each of next 2 tr and 1htr in top of turning ch, changing to **A**, turn.
Row 31[33:37:41:43:45]: Using **A**, ch2, (1htr in each htr) to end of row, 1htr in top of turning ch.
Fasten off.

Sleeves (make two)

Using 3mm (US C/2 or D/3) hook and **A**, ch88[92:96:100:104:108].
Work rows 1 to 20[20:21:21:22:22] as for back.
Fasten off.

Join shoulders

Join both shoulders by matching the stripes and the markers on the back and working a row of dc through both layers using **A**. The seam is on the outside of the work which is now the RS of your work. Place markers 19[20:21:22: 23:24]cm (7½ [7¾:8¼:8¾:9:9½] in) down from shoulder at sides on back and both fronts to show start of armholes.

Collar

With RS facing, using 3mm (US C/2 or D/3) hook and **A**, rejoin yarn 2cm (¾ in) from right front edge, work ch1 (counts as a st), then 25[25:27:27:29:29] dc up right front neck, 33[33:37:37:41:41] dc across back neck, 25dc down left front neck ending 2cm (¾ in) from left front edge, turn. 84[84:92:92:100:100] and work collar as follows:
Next row: Using **B**, ch3, 2tr in 1st dc, ch1, (miss next 3 dc, 3tr in next dc, ch1) to last 3 sts, miss 2 dc, 1tr in turning ch, turn.
Next row: Using **B**, ch3, 2tr into 1st ch1-sp, ch1, (3tr, ch1) in every sp to end of row, 1tr in top of ch3, turn.
Next row: Using **B**, ch3, 2tr into 1st ch1-sp, ch1, (3tr, ch1) in every sp to end of row, 1tr in top of ch3, changing to **A**, turn.
Next row: Using **A**, ch2, (1htr in next ch-sp, 1htr into each of next 3 tr) to last 3 sts, 1htr in next 2 tr and 1htr in top of ch3, changing to **B**, turn.
Next row: Using **B**, ch3, 2tr in 1st htr, ch1 (miss 3 htr, 3tr in next htr, ch1) to last 3 sts, miss 2 sts and work 1tr in top of turning ch, changing to **A**, turn.
Next row: Using **A**, ch2, (1htr in 1st ch-sp, 1htr into each of next 3 tr) to last 3 sts, 1htr in next 2 tr and 1htr in top of ch3, changing to **B**, turn.
Next row: Using **B**, ch2, 1htr in each htr to end of row, turn.
Next row: Using **B**, ch3, 1tr in each htr to end of row, changing to **A** turn.
Next row: Using **A**, ch2, 1htr in each tr to end of row.
Fasten off.

To finish

Weave in any yarn ends.
Pin sleeves between markers with wrong sides together. Using **A** rejoin yarn with ch1 and work a row of dc through both layers so the seam is on the RS of your work. Join side and sleeve seams using the same method, leaving 5cm (2 in) open at bottom edge to make side vents.
Sew buttons on right front, evenly spaced. The buttonholes are the spaces between blocks on the left front.

Masterclass

Using slip stitch to travel along a row

Slip stitch is a way of moving along a row of crochet but without adding any extra height to your work. Here it's used at the neck edge of the polo shirt to unobtrusively reduce the number of stitches in the rows and create a neat opening.

One   Work a slip stitch directly into the first stitch of the row where you will be decreasing – there is no need to make a turning chain.

Two   Continue working slip stitches into the top of the previous row until you have made the number given in the pattern or you reach the point where you want to continue with tall stitches.

Three   Make the number of standing chain required for the stitch you are using, then continue crocheting to the end of the row. There is now a small step at the top corner of your work.

INTERMEDIATE

Motif Vest

Believe it or not, this fashion-forward vest is made from old t-shirts for the ultimate in upcycling chic. Dig out any worn-out, un-loved or out-grown cotton t-shirts and simply cut them into continuous strips to create your own yarn. Crochet lots of individual motifs with a big hook, then lay them out using a favourite t-shirt or vest as a template, pin in place and oversew together.
I love the idea that a t-shirt that I have worn and loved can be given a new life as something completely different.

Sizing guidance
This project is made up of individual motifs, and is a little free-form. For larger or smaller sizes, you will need to make more or fewer motifs and experiment with their placement, using a t-shirt as a template. The below measurements are a guide only. The number of motifs listed are for the S/M size. Fewer motifs will be needed for the XS size and more will be needed for the larger sizes.

What you will need
- Lightweight t-shirts in assorted colours, cut into strips and wound into balls (see page 127).

Quantity:
- Approx. 640[700:770:850:930:1025]g (22½[24¾:27:29:32¾:36] oz) total weight of yarn
- 12mm (US 00) crochet hook
- Stitch marker
- 10mm (US 00) circular needle, 40cm (16 in) lengths

Abbreviations
See page 61.
Bobble (motif 5): 5tr into next dc until 1 loop of each remains on hook, yrh and draw through all 6 loops on hook.
Bobble (motif 12): 3dtr into next dc until 1 loop of each remains on hook, yrh and draw through all 4 loops on hook.

Special technique
Making your own yarn from fabric (see page 127).

Adult size	XS	S/M	L/XL	XXL	XXXL	XXXXL	
Suggested actual chest	90	100	110	120	130	140	cm
	35½	39¼	43¼	47¼	51¼	55	in
Suggested length	50	54	58	58	62	62	cm
	19¾	21¼	22¾	22¾	24½	24½4	in

Crochet Garments

To make

Motifs

Motif 1: Gemini spoke (make 4)
Approx. 18cm (7 in) in diameter
Base ring: Ch8, join with sl st.
Round 1: Ch1, 16dc into ring, sl st to 1st dc.
Round 2: Ch6 (counts as 1tr and ch3), miss next dc, (1tr in next dc, ch3, miss 1 dc) 7 times, sl st to 3rd of ch6.
Round 3: Ch1, 1dc in same place as last sl st, (4tr in next ch3-sp, 1dc in next tr] 7 times, 4tr in next ch3 -sp, sl st to 1st dc.
Fasten off.

Motif 2: Large gardenia bloom (make 2)
Approx. 20cm (7¾ in) in diameter
Base ring: Ch5, join with sl st.
Round 1: Ch6 (counts as 1tr and ch3), (1tr in ring, ch3) 5 times, sl st to 3rd of ch6.
Round 2: Ch1, 1dc in sl st, *(1tr, ch1, 1tr, ch1, 1tr) in next ch3-sp, 1dc in next tr, rep from * 5 times more missing dc at end of last rep, sl st to 1st dc.
Round 3: Ch1, 1dc in 1st dc, *ch1, miss 1tr, (1tr, ch1) 5 times into next tr, miss 1tr, 1dc into next dc, rep from * 5 times more missing dc at end of last rep, sl st to 1st dc.
Fasten off.

Motif 3: Medium gardenia bloom (make 2)
Approx. 15cm (6 in) in diameter
Base ring: Ch5, join with sl st.
Round 1: Ch6 (counts as 1tr and ch3), (1tr in ring, ch3) 5 times, sl st to 3rd of ch6.
Round 2: Ch1, 1dc into sl st, *(1tr, ch1, 1tr, ch1, 1tr) in next ch3-sp, 1dc in next tr, rep from * 5 times more missing dc at end of last rep, sl st to 1st dc.
Fasten off.

Motif 4: Small gardenia bloom (make 2)
Approx. 8cm (3¼ in) in diameter
Base ring: Ch5, join with sl st.
Round 1: Ch6 (counts as 1tr and ch3), (1tr in ring, ch3) 5 times, sl st to 3rd of ch6.
Fasten off.

Motif 5: Canterbury bell (make 6)
Approx. 12cm (4¾ in) in diameter
Base ring: Ch6, join with sl st.
Round 1: Ch1, 12dc in ring, sl st to 1st dc.
Round 2: Ch3, 4tr in same st as last sl st until 1 loop of each tr remains on hook, yrh and draw through all 5 loops on hook (1 bobble made at beg of round), *ch5, miss 1dc, 1 bobble in next dc, rep from * 4 times more, ch5, sl st to top of 1st bobble.
Fasten off.

Motif 6: Orchid blossom with short legs (make 2)
Approx. 18cm (7 in) in diameter
Base ring: Ch6, join with sl st.
Petal: (Ch6, 1dc in 2nd ch from hook, 1htr in next ch, 1tr in next ch, 1htr in next ch, 1dc in next ch, sl st in ring) 6 times.
Fasten off.

Motif 7: Orchid blossom with long legs (make 2)
Approx. 20cm (7¾ in) in diameter
Base ring: Ch6, join with sl st.
Petal: (Ch8, 1dc in 2nd ch from hook, 1htr in next ch, 1tr in next ch3, 1htr in next ch, 1dc in next ch, sl st in ring) 6 times.
Fasten off.

Motif 8: Pinwheel with 10 legs (make 1)
Approx. 16cm (6¼ in) in diameter
Base ring: Ch8, join with sl st.
Round 1: Ch1, (1dc, ch12) 10 times in ring, sl st to 1st dc.
Fasten off.

Motif 9: Pinwheel with 8 legs (make 2)
Approx. 14cm (5½ in) in diameter
Base ring: Ch8, join with sl st.
Round 1: Ch1, (1dc, ch12) 8 times in ring, sl st to 1st dc.
Fasten off.

Motif 10: Pinwheel with 6 legs (make 12)
Approx. 13cm (5 in) in diameter
Base ring: Ch6, join with sl st.
Round 1: Ch1, (1dc, ch4) 6 times in ring, sl st to 1st dc.
Fasten off.

Motif 11: Pinwheel with 8 different length legs (make 2)
Adjustable size
Base ring: Ch8, join with sl st.
Round 1: Ch1, (1dc, ch12) twice, (1dc, ch10) twice, (1dc, ch8) once, (1dc, ch6) twice and (1dc, ch4) once, sl st to 1st dc. Fasten off.

Motif 12: Four petal flower (make 2)
Approx. 8cm (3¼ in) in diameter
Base ring: Ch5, join with sl st.
Round 1: Ch1, 12dc in ring, sl st in 1st dc.
Round 2: *Ch4, 1 bobble in next dc, ch4, sl st in each of next 2 dc, rep from * 3 times more, missing 1 sl st at end of last rep, ch7, 1dc in 2nd ch from hook, 1dc in each of next ch5, sl st in 1st dc on 1st round. Fasten off.

Neckband

Knitted separately and attached after body of vest has been finished.
Using 10mm (US 15) circular needle, cast on 52[56:60:64:68:72] sts, place marker to show start of round, and work 5 rounds in k1, p1 rib, ending at marker.
Cast off loosely in rib.

To finish

Make a paper pattern of your favourite sleeveless t-shirt or vest or use the actual garment as the template. Pin the motifs to the front. You may need to crochet a few extra smaller motifs to fill in any big spaces.

Sew the motifs together using the t-shirt strips in any colour, knotting lengths together as you work. You can also use the ends left after fastening off each motif for sewing up. Repeat for the back. Then join the shoulders and the side seams.

Pin neckband in place, easing fit around neckline and whip stitch onto vest. Weave in any unused ends.

Masterclass

Making your own yarn from fabric

Both crochet and knitting can be worked using any continuous length of yarn, and that includes strips of t-shirt fabric as used here. There's no need to be painstakingly accurate when cutting up the t-shirts, just keep the strips no more than 1cm (⅜ inch) wide.

One Take each t-shirt and cut off the neckband, sleeves and hem. Next, cut along the shoulders and sides seams so that you have two flat pieces of fabric.

Two Lay the fabric out so that it is as wrinkle-free as possible. Starting at one corner of the fabric, cut along one side 1cm (⅜ inch) in from the edge, but stopping when you are 1cm (⅜ inch) from the end.

Three Next, make another cut in the opposite direction, 1cm (⅜ inch) from the previous cut and again stopping before you reach the end of the fabric. Continue making cuts in this way across the whole surface of the fabric. This will make one continuous 1cm (⅜ inch) wide length of fabric in a sort of spiral.

Four Join all the lengths of t-shirt fabric together with a simple knot and wind into balls of separate colours. Now it's ready to be crocheted.

Crochet Garments

EASY

Random Stripe Sweater

This wide, cropped t-shirt-style sweater makes a feature of the knotted ends of the colour changes. A brilliant stash-buster project, the random colour stripe – which varies each time – is achieved simply by knotting different lengths together. This project is all about celebrating the making process.

Measurements
See chart below. Sweater to be worn with approx. 11cm (4¼ in) to 26cm (10¼ in) ease.

What you will need
- Kremke Soul Wool Morning Salutation 51% lyocell, 49% cotton, 110m (120 yards) per 50g (1¾ oz)

Quantity:
- **A** 3[3:4:4:4:5] x 50g (1¾ oz) balls in Blue
- **B** 3[3:4:4:4:5] x 50g (1¾ oz) balls in Indigo
- **C** 3[3:4:4:4:5] x 50g (1¾ oz) balls in Pink
- **D** 3[3:4:4:4:5] x 50g (1¾ oz) balls in Gold
- **E** 4[4:5:5:6:6] x 50g (1¾ oz) balls in Jade
- 3.5mm (US E/4) crochet hook
- 4mm (US G/6) crochet hook
- 5mm (US H/8) crochet hook
- 3.75mm (US 5) circular knitting needle, 40cm (16 in) length
- Stitch markers
- Yarn needle

Tension (gauge)
15 sts and 13 rows to 10cm (4 in) over htr on 4mm (US G/6) hook, or size required to achieve the correct tension (gauge).

Abbreviations
See page 61.
Inc work 2htr in first st. 1 st inc.
Dec work htr2tog over next 2 sts. 1 st dec.

Special technique
Winding yarn for stripes (see page 133).

Notes
The sweater is crocheted edge to edge in htr throughout and is finished with a knitted ribbed neckband and cuffs.
The foundation row is the RS for this pattern.

Adult size	XS	S/M	L/XL	XXL	XXXL	XXXXL	
Actual chest	107.5	117	126	138	147.5	160	cm
	42½	46	49½	54½	58	63	in
Length (from side seam)	54	57	58	61	62	65	cm
	21¼	22½	22¾	24	24½	25½	in
Sleeve length	21	22	23	23	24	25	cm
	8¼	8¾	9	9	9½	10	in

To make

Prepare the yarn
Before starting work, cut the yarn into various lengths and then randomly knot them together. Wind the knotted lengths into one multi-coloured ball (see page 133). Each garment will be unique. You can leave the knotted ends showing on the RS or push them through to the WS to hide them.

For the back, take one ball of each colour and from each cut the following lengths:
1 x 7m (8 yards)
2 x 15m (17 yards)
2 x 22m (24 yards)
1 x 28m (31 yards)

Repeat for the front but start using any leftover yarn from the first ball.

For each sleeve, take one ball of each colour and from each cut the following lengths:
1 x 2m (3 yards)
2 x 4m (5 yards)
2 x 6m (7 yards)
1 x 8m (9 yards)

Back

Using 5mm (US H/8) hook, ch83[87:89:93:95:99].
Change to 4mm (US G/6) hook.
Foundation row (RS): 1htr in 3rd ch from hook, 1htr in each ch to end, turn. *81[85:87:91:93:97] htr.*
Row 1: Ch2 (not counted as st here and throughout), 1htr in each st to end, turn.

Shape right shoulder
**Sizes XS, S/M and L/XL only
Row 2 (RS inc): Ch2, 2htr in 1st st (shoulder edge), 1htr in each st to end, turn. *82[86:88:–:–:–] sts.*
Row 3: Ch2, 1htr in each st to end, turn.
Row 4: Ch2, 1htr in each st to end, turn.
Row 5 (inc): Ch2, 1htr in each st to last st, 2htr in last st (shoulder edge), turn. *83[87:89:–:–:–] sts.*
Inc as above at shoulder edge on every following 3rd row 5 times more. *88[92:94:–:–:–] sts.*
Sizes S/M and L/XL only
Next row: Ch2, 1htr in each st to end, turn.
Next row: Ch2, 1htr in each st to end, turn.
Repeat last 2 rows –[0:1:–:–:–] times more, placing a marker to show end of shoulder shaping.
Sizes XXL and XXXL only
Row 2 (RS inc): Ch2, 2htr in 1st st (shoulder edge), 1htr in each st to end, turn. *–[–:–:92:94:–] sts.*
Row 3: Ch2, 1htr in each st to end, turn.
Repeat last row twice more.
Row 6 (inc): Ch2, 2htr in 1st st (shoulder edge), 1htr in each st to end, turn. *–[–:–:93:95:–] sts.*
Inc as above at shoulder edge on every following 4th row 5 times more. *–[–:–:98:100:–] sts.*
Next row: Ch2, 1htr in each st to end, turn.
Next row: Ch2, 1htr in each st to end, turn.
Repeat last 2 rows –[–:–:0:1:–] times more.
Sizes XXXXL only
Row 2 (RS inc): Ch2, 2htr in 1st st (shoulder edge), 1htr in each st to end, turn. *–[–:–:–:–:98] sts.*
Row 3: Ch2, 1htr in each st to end, turn.
Row 4: Ch2, 1htr in each st to end, turn.
Repeat last 2 rows once more.
Row 7 (inc): Ch2, 1htr in each st to last st, 2htr in last st (shoulder edge), turn. *–[–:–:–:–:99] sts.*
Inc as above at shoulder edge on every following 5th row 5 times more. *–[–:–:–:–:104] sts.*
Next row: Ch2, 1htr in each st to end, turn.
Next row: Ch2, 1htr in each st to end, turn.
All sizes
88[92:94:98:100:104] sts.
Place marker to show end of shoulder shaping.**

Back neck
Work 28[30:32:32:34:34] rows straight, ending with WS facing for next row, turn, placing marker at shoulder edge of last row.
Work 0[2:4:2:4:2] rows straight.

***Shape left shoulder
Sizes XS, S/M and L/XL only
Next row (dec): Ch2, 1htr in each st to last 2 sts, htr2tog over last 2 sts (shoulder edge), turn. *87[91:93:–:–:–] sts.*
Work 2 rows straight.
Next row: Ch2, htr2tog over next 2 sts (shoulder edge), 1htr in each st to end, turn. *86[90:93:–:–:–] sts.*
Dec as above at shoulder edge on every following 3rd row 5 times more. *81[85:87:–:–:–] sts.*
Work 2 rows straight.
Sizes XXL and XXXL only
Next row (dec): Ch2, 1htr in each st to last 2 sts, htr2tog over these last 2 sts (shoulder edge), turn. *–[–:–:97:99:–] sts.*
Work 3 rows straight.
Next row: Ch2, 1htr in each st to last 2 sts, htr2tog over these last 2 sts (shoulder edge), turn. *–[–:–:96:98:–] sts.*
Dec as above st shoulder edge on every following 4th row 5 times more. *–[–:–:91:93:–] sts.*
Work 2 rows straight.
Sizes XXXXL only
Next row (dec): Ch2, 1htr in each st to last 2 sts, htr2tog over these last 2 sts (shoulder edge), turn. *–[–:–:–:–:103] sts.*
Work 4 rows straight.
Next row: Ch2, htr2tog over next 2 sts (shoulder edge), htr in each st to end, turn. *–[–:–:–:–:102] sts.*
Dec at shoulder edge on every following 5th row 5 times more. *–[–:–:–:–:97] sts.*
Work 2 rows straight.
All sizes
Fasten off.***

Front

Using 5mm (US H/8) hook, ch83[87:89:93:95:99].
Change to 4mm (US G/6) hook.
Foundation row (RS): 1htr in 3rd ch from hook, 1htr in each ch to end, turn. *81[85:87:91:93:97] sts.*
Row 1: Ch2 (not counted as st here and throughout), 1htr in each st to end, turn.

Shape left shoulder
Work as given for right shoulder on back from ** to **, ending with WS facing for next row. *88[92:94:98:100:104] sts.*

Shape neck
Next row (2 st dec): Ch2, 1htr in each st to last 2 sts, turn. *86[90:92:96:98:102] sts.*
Dec 1 st at neck edge on next 8 rows. *78[82:84:88:90:94] sts.*
Work 10[12:14:14:16:16] rows straight, ending with RS facing for next row.
Inc 1 st at neck edge on next 8 rows. *86[90:92:96:98:102] sts.*
Next row (RS, 2 sts inc): Ch2, 2htr in 1st st, 1htr in each st to end, turn. *88[92:94:98:100:104] sts.*
Work 0[2:4:2:4:2] rows straight.

Shape right shoulder
Work as given for left shoulder on back from *** to ***.

Sleeves (make 2 the same)
Using 5mm (US H/8) hook and ball made for sleeves, ch27[29:31:31:33:33].
Change to 4mm (US G/6) hook.
Foundation row (RS): 1htr in 3rd ch from hook, 1htr in each ch to end, turn. *25[27:29:29:31:31] sts.*
Row 1: Ch2 (not counted as st here and throughout), 1htr in each st to end, turn.
Repeat last row until sleeve meas 38[40:42:44:46:48]cm (15[16:16½:17¼:18:19] in).
Fasten off.

To finish

Join both shoulders with WS of work tog by matching markers on back with front shoulders using 3.5mm (US E/4) hook and any colour rejoin yarn at start of shoulder and work as follows:
Ch1, then work row of dc through both layers. The seam is on the outside (RS) of work.
Place markers 19[20:21:22:23:24]cm (7½[8:8¼:8¾:9:9½] in) down from shoulder on back and front to show start of armholes.

Pin the sleeves between armhole markers with WS tog. Rejoin any colour yarn, ch1, work row of dc through both layers.
The seam is on the outside (RS) of work. Join the side and sleeve seams using the same method.

Neckband

With RS facing, 3.75mm (US 5) circular knitting needle and **B**, and starting at left shoulder, pick up and knit 15 sts down left front neck, 18[18:22:22:24:24] sts across front neck, 15 sts up right front neck and 44[46:52:52:54:54] sts across back neck, place marker to show start of round.
92[92:104:104:108:108] sts.
Work in k1, p1 rib in rounds in the following colours:
10 rounds **B**, ending at marker.
2 rounds **A**, ending at marker.
9 rounds **B**, ending at marker.
Cast off (bind off) in rib.

Cuffs

With RS facing, 3.75mm (US 5) circular knitting needle and **B**, and starting at underarm seam, pick up and knit 80[84:88:92:96:100] sts evenly around sleeve, place marker to show start of round.
Work in k1, p1 rib in rounds in the following colours:
5 rows **B**, ending at marker.
2 rows **A**, ending at marker.
4 rows **B**, ending at marker.
Cast off (bind off) in rib.

Only weave in the yarn ends used for joining the garment and knitting the collar and cuffs.
Leave the knots made when making up the balls of yarn at the start of your work to show on the outside (RS) of the sweater.

Masterclass

Winding yarn for stripes

This method of cutting up and then rejoining coloured yarns creates random stripes as you work, meaning that no two versions of this pattern will ever be the same. Your garment will be utterly unique to you. Once you've completed your project, you can either leave the knotted ends showing on the outside (right side) of the garment or poke them through to the inside (wrong side) to hide them.

Cut your chosen yarns into various lengths. Using a simple overhand knot, randomly tie two different coloured lengths of yarn together. Wind the knotted yarns into one multi-coloured ball ready to start crocheting.

Crochet Homewar

-05

es

EASY

Plant Pots

We have houseplants all over our home as I'm a real plant lover. I love the idea of making woolly pot covers for them. They're made using three strands of yarn held together to create a super chunky colour-marl effect and in a crochet stitch that mimics a knit stitch. You'll soon find other uses for these practical pot holders – keeping pens and crayons tidy on your desk, storing keys and other bits and bobs by the front door, or even holding your cosmetics on your dressing table.

Measurements
Small: Approx. 10cm (4 in) diameter x 9cm (3½ in) tall
Medium: Approx. 12cm (4¾ in) diameter x 12cm (4¾ in) tall
Large: Approx. 18cm (7 in) diameter x 16cm (6¾ in) tall

What you will need
- Wool Couture Cheeky Chunky 100% merino wool, 65m (71 yards) per 100g (3½ oz)

Quantity:
Small
- **A** 1 x 100g (3½ oz) ball in Natural Cream
- **B** 1 x 100g (3½ oz) ball in Black

Medium
- **B** 1 x 100g (3½ oz) ball in Black
- **C** 1 x 100g (3½ oz) ball in Raspberry
- **D** 1 x 100g (3½ oz) ball in Mustard

Large
- **B** 1 x 100g (3½ oz) ball in Black
- **D** 1 x 100g (3½ oz) ball in Mustard
- **E** 1 x 100g (3½ oz) ball in Cinnamon
- 20mm (US S) crochet hook
- Stitch marker
- Yarn needle

Tension (gauge)
5 sts and 6 rows to 10cm (4 in) over patt with three yarn strands held together on 20mm (US S) hook, or size required to achieve the correct tension (gauge).

Abbreviations
See page 61.

Special techniques
Working the knit stitch (also called waistcoat stitch, see page 87).
This stitch is just like a regular dc but instead of working the dc into the top two loops of the dc, it is worked through the two front vertical posts of the dc.

Notes
Three strands of yarn are held together for each pot. The small pot is made with two strands of A and one strand of B held together. The medium and large pots are made with one strand of each of the three colours held together.
All pots are worked in a continuous round. Place a marker on the last st of each round and move it up as you work.

To make

Small pot

Using 2 strands of **A** and 1 of **B** held together, ch4 and join with a sl st in 1st ch to form a ring.
Foundation row (RS): Ch1, 6dc in ring, place marker on last dc. *6 sts.*
Round 1: 2dc in each st to end of round. *12 sts.*
Round 2: 1dc in each st to end of round. Continue in knit stitch (see Notes on page 137) as follows:
Round 3: 1 knit st in each st to end of round.
Repeat last round 4 times more.
Fasten off.

Medium pot

Using 1 strand each of **B**, **C** and **D** held together, ch4 and join with a sl st in 1st ch to form a ring.
Foundation round (RS): Ch1, 6dc in ring, place marker on last dc. *6 sts.*
Round 1: 2dc in each st to end of round. *12 sts.*
Round 2: *1dc in next st, 2dc in next st, rep from * to end of round. *18 sts.*
Round 3: 1dc in each st to end of round. Continue in knit stitch (see Notes on page 137) as follows:
Round 4: 1 knit st in each st to end of round.
Repeat last round 6 times more.
Fasten off.

Large pot

Using 1 strand each of **B**, **D** and **E** held together, ch4 and join with a sl st in 1st ch to form a ring.
Foundation round (RS): Ch1, 6dc in ring, place marker on last dc. *6 sts.*
Round 1: 2dc in each st to end of round. *12 sts.*
Round 2: *1dc in next st, 2dc in next st, rep from * to end of round. *18 sts.*
Round 3: *1dc in each of next 2 sts, 2dc in next st, rep from * to end of round. *24 sts.*
Round 4: 1dc in each st to end of round. Continue in knit stitch (see Notes on page 137) as follows:
Round 5: 1 knit st in each st to end of round.
Repeat last round 9 times more.
Fasten off.

To finish all sizes

Weave in any yarn ends.

Masterclass

Working with two or more yarns at the same time

You can create interesting colours or textural effects in your knitting or crochet by using two or more yarns held together at the same time as if you were knitting or crocheting with a single yarn. You simply hold the yarns together as one and get going with your pattern as usual. For the best results, always work a tension or gauge swatch first so you know exactly how many stitches you need and which size needles or hook to use for your chosen pattern. Remember that using more than one yarn at a time will change the weight of yarn, making it thicker. In terms of yarn size, this is a rough guide:

- Two strands of super fine weight (1) = one strand of fine weight (2)
- Two strands of fine weight (2) = one strand of light worsted weight (3)
- Two strands of light worsted weight (3) = one strand of worsted weight (4)
- Two strands of worsted weight (4) = one strand of bulky weight (5)
- Two strands of bulky weight (5) = one strand of super bulky (6)

If you knit or crochet with two yarns of contrasting colour, you will be left with a speckled or tweedy looking fabric and this effect is called marl. This can be used to emphasise shape and form because it can add real depth to your fabric and you can also create ombre patterns. You can also turn any regular pattern into a marled effect by using two thinner strands of yarn, so the result has the same gauge as the original pattern. Mix and match different colours to get the results that you love the look of.

A contrast in texture of the yarns can create interesting results too, so you can add a fluffy mohair yarn to a smooth wool yarn or a silky yarn with a novelty yarn – the combinations are endless.

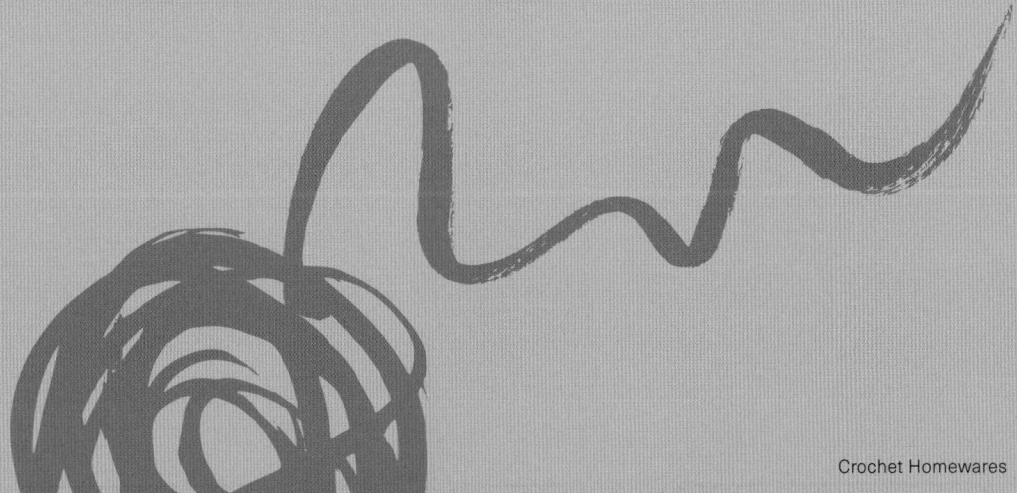

EASY

Shaggy Cushion

Is it a woolly monster? Is it a fluffy pet? No, it's a cushion! Brighten up your space with this bold and fun homeware item. It has a retro feel with shaggy fringes in random patches of colour to add textural interest and is a great way to add a splash of colour to your living space without investing in all-new decoration. It might look complicated, but this is a great beginner's crochet project. What are you waiting for?

Measurements
One size
Approx. 60cm (23¾ in) x 60cm (23¾ in)

What you will need
- MWL The Chunky One
  100% merino wool
  65m (71 yards) per 100g (3½ oz)

Quantity:
- **A** 8 x 100g (3½ oz) balls in Black
- **B** 1 x 100g (3½ oz) balls in Damson
- **C** 1 x 100g (3½ oz) balls in Raspberry
- **D** 1 x 100g (3½ oz) balls in Aquamarine
- **E** 1 x 100g (3½ oz) balls in Oxford Blue

- 10mm (US N/15) crochet hook
- 60cm (23¾ in) square cushion pad (pillow insert)
- Yarn needle

Tension (gauge)
Approx. (5dc + ch1) and 10 rows to 10cm (4 in) over patt using 10mm (US N/15) hook, or size required to achieve the correct tension (gauge).

Abbreviations
See page 61.

To make

Back and front
(both alike)

Using 10mm (US N/15) hook and **A**, ch62.
Row 1 (RS): 1dc in 3rd ch from hook, *1ch, miss next ch, 1dc in next ch, rep from * to end of row, turn.
Row 2: 1ch (counts as 1st dc), 1dc in 1st ch1-sp, *1ch, 1dc in next ch1-sp, rep from * to last sp, 1ch, 1dc in turning ch, turn.
Repeat Row 2 until work meas 60cm (23¾ in).
Fasten off.

To finish

Weave in any yarn ends.

Add fringing
(on one side of cushion only)

Add to one side of cushion only, using the photographs as a guide to colour placement, or create your own pattern. Cut scraps of contrast colour yarns (**B**, **C**, **D**, **E**) into lengths of approx. 22cm (8¾ in) long. For each fringe, take a length of yarn and fold in half. Push crochet hook horizontally through the first dc. Using the crochet hook pull the folded yarn down half-way through the stitch, then take the loop and pull the ends through to secure. Repeat in random patches of colour using the photograph as a guide, if you wish. Trim each fringe to neaten to approx 10cm (4 in), or as desired.

With RS of work together, pin around three sides. Backstitch round these three sides being careful not to catch the loops in the seam as you work. Turn RS out. Insert the cushion pad (pillow insert) and join the final seam with whip stitch.

INTERMEDIATE

Alphabet Bunting

Handmade bunting adds a heartfelt touch. Here's an entire alphabet of lower-case letters, plus a cute heart motif, that can be crocheted individually or in multiples to combine into bunting for any occasion. Imagine 'happy birthday to you' in crochet letters pegged onto a string for family birthdays – whether draped across the wall at a kid's party or strung between two trees in the park for an outdoor gathering. But don't stop there – choose a single letter, or a whole word, and add to a gift tag, make into a keyring, or appliqué onto a sweater, t-shirt, or cushion for a really personal touch.

Measurements
Letters Approx. 11cm (4¼ in) tall
Heart Approx. 8cm (3¼ in) tall

What you will need
- Kremke Soul Wool Karma Cotton
  70% cotton, 30% recycled polyamide
  105m (115 yards) per 50g (1¾ oz)

Quantity:
- **A** 1 x 50g (1¾ oz) ball in Orange (04)
- **B** 1 x 50g (1¾ oz) ball in Aquamarine (15)
- **C** 1 x 50g (1¾ oz) ball in Violet (19)
- **D** 1 x 50g (1¾ oz) ball in Lime (09)
- **E** 1 x 50g (1¾ oz) ball in Deep Pink (06)
- **F** 1 x 50g (1¾ oz) ball in Yellow (02)
- 4mm (US G/6) crochet hook
- Yarn needle

Tension (gauge)
An exact tension (gauge) is not critical for this project.

Abbreviations
See page 61.

To make

Individual letters

a

Foundation row: Ch49, turn.
Round 1: Working in 2nd st from hook, 7dc, (sk1, 1dc) 5 times, 29dc, 3dc in end st, now work along other side of foundation chain, 45dc, 2dc in last st, ch1, turn.
Round 2: Working in 2nd st from hook, 6dc, (2dc in next st, 1dc) 6 times, 6dc, sl1, ch5, working in 2nd st from hook, 4dc, start working in dc next to bottom of ch5, 7dc, (2dc in next st, 1dc) 5 times, 2dc (2dc in next st) 3 times, 4dc, (sk1, 1dc) 4 times, sl1 through next st and through 1st st of crossbar of "a" (this is at beg of row as it curls into place), making sure work is not twisted. Do not turn.
Round 3: 29dc, sl1, 2dc, (2dc in next st) 3 times, 16dc, (2dc in next st, 1dc) twice, 9dc, (2dc in next st) 3 times, sk1, sl1, cut yarn and draw through loop on hook to finish. Sew row ends of crossbar in place.

b

Foundation row: Ch24, join to first dc with a sl st, ch1.
Round 1: 24dc, join to first ch with a sl st, ch7, turn.
Round 2: Working in 2nd st from hook, 6dc along ch7, 6dc, (2dc in next st, 1dc) 3 times, 7dc, (2dc in next st, 1dc) 3 times, sk1.
Round 3: Sl2, (working along ch7) 4dc, 3dc in end st, 35dc, sk1.
Round 4: Sk2, 3dc, (2dc in next st) 3 times, 13dc, ch5, working in 2nd st from hook, 3dc, sk1, sl1, 2dc, (2dc in next st, 1dc) 3 times, 2dc in next st, 6dc, (2dc in next st, 1dc) 3 times, sl1, sk1, 4dc, (2dc in next st) 3 times, 17dc, 3dc in end st, sk1, sl1, 28dc, sk1, sl1, cut yarn and draw through loop on hook to finish.

c

Foundation row: Ch34, turn.
Round 1: working into 2nd st from hook, dc32, dc3 into next st, dc32, dc3 into end st, dc1, (sk1, dc1) 7 times, dc6, (sk1, dc1) 7 times, dc3 into next st
Round 2: dc3, (dc2 into next st, dc1) twice, dc19, (dc2 into next st, dc1) twice, dc2, dc2 into next 3 sts
Round 3: dc19, dc2 into next 3 sts, dc37, dc2 into next 3 sts, slip 1, cut yarn and draw through loop on hook to finish.

Foundation row: Ch34, turn.
Round 1: Working in 2nd st from hook, 32dc, 3dc in next st, now work along other side of foundation chain, 32dc, 3dc in end st, 1dc, (sk1, 1dc) 7 times, 6dc, (sk1, 1dc) 7 times, 3dc in next st.
Round 2: 3dc, (2dc in next st, 1dc) twice, 19dc, (2dc in next st, 1dc) twice, 3dc, 2dc in next 3 sts.
Round 3: 20dc, 2dc in next 3 sts, 37dc, 2dc in next 3 sts, sl1, cut yarn and draw through loop on hook to finish.

d

Foundation row: Ch24, join to first ch with sl1.
Round 1: 24dc, ch1, (2dc in next st, 1dc) 12 times, sl1 in ch1 at beg of round.
Round 2: 36dc, sl2, ch9, working in 2nd st from hook, 7dc, sk1, sl1 in next st of previous round, (2dc in next st, 2dc) 9 times, sl1, ch5, working in 2nd st from hook, 3dc, sl1 in next st of previous row, 6dc.
Round 3: Working along ch9, sk1, 6dc, 3dc in end st, 5dc, sk2, sl1, 30dc, sk1, sl1, sk2, 2dc, 3dc in end st, 3dc, sk1, sl1, 11dc, (2dc in next st) 3 times, 4dc, sk2, sl2, [5dc, (2dc in next st, 2dc) twice] twice, 10dc, sl1, cut yarn and draw through loop on hook to finish.

e

Foundation row: Ch47, turn.
Round 1: Working in 2nd stitch from hook, 7dc, (sk1, 1dc) 5 times, 29dc, 3dc in end st, now work along other side of foundation chain, 46dc, 2dc in last st, ch1, turn.
Round 2: Working in 2nd st from hook, 6dc, (2dc in next st, 1dc) 6 times, 27dc, (2dc in next st) 3 times, 1dc, (sk1, 1dc) 9 times, sl1 through next st and 1st st of crossbar of

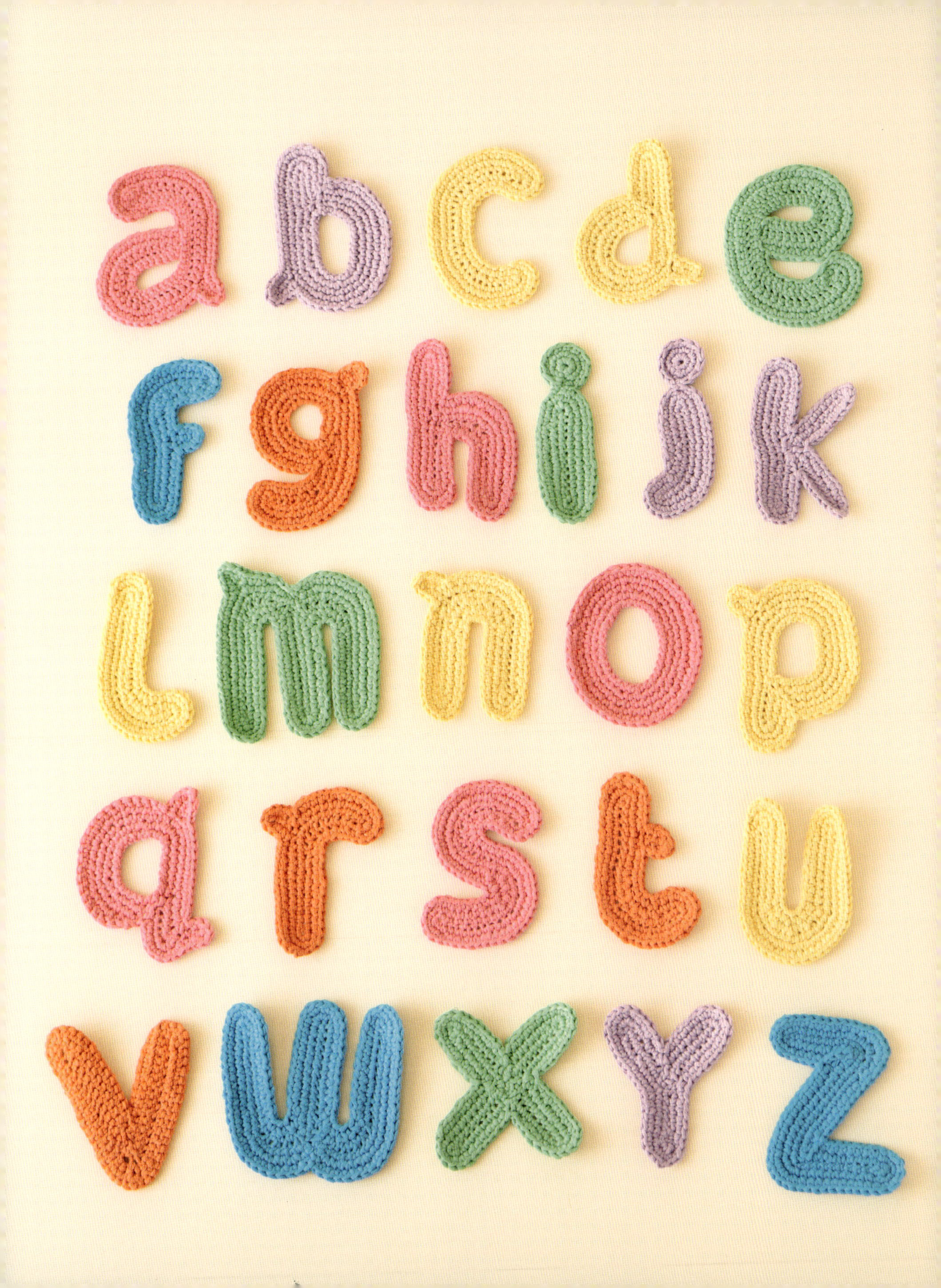

a b c d e
f g h i j k
l m n o p
q r s t u
v w x y z

"e", making sure work is not twisted.
Round 3: 40dc, (2dc in next st, 1dc) 6 times, (2dc in next st) 3 times, dc through next st and 7th st of crossbar of "e" with a sl st, cut yarn and draw through loop on hook to finish.
Sew row ends of crossbar in place.

f

Foundation row: Ch24, turn.
Round 1: Working in 2nd st from hook, 22dc, 3dc in end st, now work along other side of foundation chain, 22dc, 3dc in end st.
Round 2: 8dc, ch5, working in 2nd st from hook, 3dc, sl1, 1dc in st next to ch5, 1dc, (sk1, 1dc) 6 times, (2dc in next st) 3 times, 22dc, (2dc in next st) 3 times, 6dc, sl1, sk1, 3dc, 3dc in end st, 2dc, sl1, sk1, 3dc, sk1, 1dc, sk1, sl1, cut yarn and draw through loop on hook to finish.

g

Foundation row: Ch45, turn.
Round 1: Working in 2nd stitch from hook, 43dc, ch1, turn, working in 3rd st from hook, 32dc, (2dc in next st, 1dc) 4 times, 2dc in next 3 sts, sl1 in 17th st from far end, making sure work is not twisted.
Round 2: 4dc, (sk1, 1dc) 5 times, 1dc, (2dc in next st) 3 times, 22dc, sl1, ch5, working in 2nd st from hook, 2dc, sk1, sl1, dc in st next to ch5, (2dc in next st, 2dc) 7 times, 2dc in next st, sk2, sl1 attaching to crossbar.
Round 3: 2dc, (sk1, 1dc) 3 times, 1dc, (2dc in next st, 1dc) twice, 5dc, (2dc in next st, 2dc) twice, 11dc, sk1, sl1, 2dc, 3dc in st at top, 2dc, sk1, 7dc, (2dc in next st, 2dc) 6 times, 3dc, sk1, sl1, cut yarn and draw through loop on hook to finish.
Sew row ends of crossbar in place.

h

Foundation row: Ch28, turn.
Round 1: Working in 2nd st from hook, 18dc, sl1, turn, 1dc in 1st st from hook, ch8, turn, working in 2nd st from hook, 7dc, 2dc in next st, 8dc (remaining foundation chs), 3dc in end st, turn, now work along other side of foundation chain, 6dc, (sk1, 1dc) 5 times, 8dc, 3dc in last st.
Round 2: 8dc, (2dc in next st, 1dc) 4 times, sk1, 6dc down other side of ch8, 3dc in end st, 7dc, sk1, 4dc, sk1, 3dc, 3dc in next 3 sts.
Round 3: 8dc, (sk1, 1dc) 3 times, 6dc, 2dc in next 3 sts, 19dc, sl1, sk1, 5dc, (2dc in next st) 3 times, 13dc, sk1, sl1, cut yarn and draw through loop on hook to finish.

i

(for "dot")
Foundation row: Ch3, join with slip st, ch1.
Round 1: 6dc in 'ring', sl st to 1st dc, ch1.
Round 2: (2dc in each st) 6 times, sl st to ch1, ch1. *12 sts.*
Round 3: 12dc, sl st to ch1, cut yarn and draw through loop on hook to finish.
(for "stem")
Foundation row: Ch14.
Round 1: Working in 2nd st from hook, 12dc, 3dc in next st, now work along other side of foundation chain, 12dc, 3dc in end st.
Round 2: 12dc, 2dc in next 3 sts, 12dc, 2dc in next 3 sts.
Round 3: 33dc, sl1, cut yarn and draw through loop on hook to finish.
Attach dot to top of stem.

j

(for "dot")
Foundation row: Ch3, join with sl st, ch1.
Round 1: 6dc in 'ring', sl st to 1st dc, ch1.
Round 2: (2dc in each st) 6 times, sl st to ch1, ch1. *12 sts.*
Round 3: 12dc, sl st to ch1, cut yarn and draw through loop on hook to finish.
(for "stem")
Foundation row: Ch16, turn.
Round 1: Working in 2nd st from hook, 14dc, 3dc in end st, now work along other side of foundation chain, 14dc, 3dc in end st.
Round 2: 3dc, 2dc in next 3 sts, 8dc, 2dc in next 3 sts, 5dc, (sk1, 1dc) 4 times, 5dc, 2dc in next 3 sts.
Round 3: 32dc, sl1, cut yarn and draw through loop on hook to finish.
Attach dot to top of stem.

k
Foundation row: Ch20, turn.
Round 1: Working in 2nd st from hook, 18dc, 3dc in last st, now work along other side of foundation chain 6dc, sl1, ch12, working in 2nd st from hook, 11dc (*), 1dc in same place last st of previous 6dc, ch13, working in 2nd st from hook, 12dc, sl1 in dc at base of last dc of 12dc (*), now work along rem ch on other side of foundation chain sk1, 9dc, 3dc in next st, 18dc, (2dc in next st) 3 times.
Round 2: 4dc, sl1, sk4, sl1, sk1, 7dc working in other side of ch, 3dc in next st, 9dc, sl1, sk4, sl1, 8dc working in other side of ch, 3dc in next st, 8dc, sl1, sk4, sl1, 8dc, (2dc in next st) 3 times, 19dc, sl1, cut yarn and draw through loop on hook to finish.

l
Foundation row: Ch24, turn.
Round 1: Working in 2nd st from hook, 22dc, 3dc in end st, now work along other side of foundation chain 22dc, 3dc in end st.
Round 2: 7dc, 2dc in next 3 sts, 12dc, (2dc in next st, 1dc) 5 times, 2dc in next 3 sts, 2dc, (sk1, 1dc) twice, 6dc, 2dc in next 3 sts, sl1, cut yarn and draw through loop on hook to finish.

m
Foundation row: Ch40, turn.
Round 1: Working in 2nd st from hook, 15dc, ch24, turn, working in 2nd st from hook, 23dc, 23dc along original foundation chain, 3dc in end stitch.
Round 2: Now work along other side of foundation chain 12dc, (sk1, 1dc) 7 times, 10dc, 3dc in end st, 12dc, (sk1, 1dc) 7 times, 12dc, 3dc in end st, 15dc, (2dc in next st, 1dc) 3 times, (1dc, sk1) twice, (1dc, 2dc in next st) 3 times, ch4, turn, working in 2nd st from hook, 3dc, dc in base of last dc before ch4, 15dc, 3dc in end st.
Round 3: 10dc, (sk1, 1dc) 5 times, 10dc, (2dc in next st) 3 times, 10dc, (sk1, 1dc) 5 times, 11dc, (2dc in next st) 3 times, 23dc, sk1, sl1, 30dc, sl1, cut yarn and draw through loop on hook to finish.

n
Foundation row: Ch36, turn.
Round 1: Working in 2nd st from hook, ch34, 3dc in next st, now work along other side of foundation chain 11dc, (2dc in next st, 1dc) 4 times, 1dc, ch5, working in 2nd st from hook, 3dc, sl1 in base of ch5, 2dc in next st, 13dc, 3dc in end st, 13dc, (sk1, 2dc) 4 times, 10dc, (2dc in next st) 3 times.
Round 2: 23dc, sl1, sk1, 3dc, 3dc in end st, 2dc, sl1, sk1, sl1, 13dc, (2dc in next st) 3 times, 10dc, (sk1, 2dc) 4 times, 10dc, sl1, cut yarn and draw through loop on hook to finish.

o
Foundation row: Ch30, join to 1st ch with sl st making sure work is not twisted, ch1.
Round 1: 30dc, join to ch1 from previous round with a sl st, ch1.
Round 2: 10dc, (2dc in next st, 1dc) 3 times, 8dc, (2dc in next st, 1dc) 3 times, sl st to 1st dc, ch1. *36 sts.*
Round 3: 36dc, sl st to 1st dc, ch1.
Round 4: (2dc into next st, 2dc) 12 times, sl st to 1st dc, ch1. *48 sts.*
Round 5: Dc to end of round, sl1, cut yarn and draw through loop on hook to finish.

p
Foundation row: Ch24, join to 1st ch with sl1.
Round 1: 24dc, ch1, (2dc in next st, 1dc) 12 times, sl1 in ch1 at beg of round.
Round 2: Sl3, ch9, working in 2nd st from hook, 7dc, sk1, sl1 in next st from previous round, (2dc in next st, 2dc) 9 times, sl1, ch5, working in 2nd st from hook, 3dc, sl1 in next st of previous row, 8dc.
Round 3: Working along ch9, 7dc, 3dc in end st, 5dc, sk2, sl1, 30dc, sk1, sl1, sk2, 2dc, 3dc in end st, 3dc, sk1, sl1, 15dc, (2dc in next st) 3 times, 4dc, sk2, sl2, [5dc, (2dc in next st, 2dc) twice] twice, 5dc, sl1, cut yarn and draw through loop on hook to finish.

q
Foundation row: Ch24, join to 1st ch with a sl st, ch1.
Round 1: 24dc, join to 1st ch with a sl st, ch7, turn.

Round 2: Sl2, (working along ch7) 4dc, 3dc in end st, 1dc, ch5, turn, working in 2nd st from hook, 3dc, sk1, sl1, 13dc, ch5, turn, working in 2nd st from hook, 3dc, sl1, sk1, sl1, 19dc, sl1, sk2, sk1, 4dc, 2dc in next 2 sts, sk1, 3dc, 3dc in next st, 2dc, sl1, sk2, sl1, 11dc, sl1, 2dc, 3dc in end st, 2dc, sl1, sk2, sl1, 3dc, (2dc in next st, 1dc) 3 times, 3dc, (2dc in next st, 1dc) 3 times, sl2, turn.
Round 4: Sk2, 21dc, sl1, cut yarn and draw through loop on hook to finish.

r
Foundation row: Ch26, turn.
Round 1: Working in 2nd st from hook, 24dc, 3dc in end st, 10dc, (sk1, 1dc) 6 times, 2dc, 3dc in end st.
Round 2: 10dc, sl1, ch5, working in 2nd st from hook, 3dc, sk1, sl1 in st next to base of ch5, 12dc, (2dc in next st) 3 times.
Round 3: 15dc, sk1, 1dc, sk1, 2dc in next 3 sts, (1dc, 2dc in next st) 4 times, sl1, sk1, 3dc, 3dc in next st, 3dc, sk1, 14dc, sl1, cut yarn and draw through loop on hook to finish.

s
Foundation row: Ch40, turn.
Round 1: Working in 2nd st from hook, 1dc, (2dc in next st, 1dc) 3 times, 23dc, (sk1, 1dc) 3 times, 2dc in last st, 8dc, (2dc in next st, 1dc) 5 times, 3dc, (sk1, 1dc) 5 times, 6dc, 3dc in last st.
Round 2: 7dc, (2dc in next st, 1dc) 4 times, 6dc, (sk1, 1dc) 4 times, 9dc, 2dc in next 3 sts.
Round 3: 26dc, (sk1, 1dc) 4 times, 4dc, 2dc in next 3 sts, 26dc, (sk1, 1dc) 4 times, 5dc, sl1, cut yarn and draw through loop on hook to finish.

t
Foundation row: Ch24, turn.
Round 1: Working in 2nd st from hook, 22dc, 3dc in end st now work along other side of foundation chain, 22dc, 3dc in end st.
Round 2: 3dc, (sk1, 1dc) 6 times, 3dc, ch5, turn, working in 2nd st from hook, 3dc, sl1, 1dc in st next to ch5, 2dc, 2dc in next 3 sts.
Round 3: 12dc, (2dc in next st, 1dc) 5 times, 2dc in next 3 sts, 2dc, (sk1, 1dc) twice, 5dc, sl1, sk1, 3dc, 3dc in end st, 2dc, sl1, sk1, 3dc, 2dc in next 3 sts, sl1, cut yarn and draw through loop on hook to finish.

u
Foundation row: Ch36, turn.
Round 1: Working in 2nd st from hook, ch34, 3dc in next st, 11dc, (2dc in next st, 1dc) 6 times, 10dc, 3dc in end st, 13dc, (sk1, 2dc) 4 times, 13dc, (2dc in next st) 3 times.
Round 2: 40dc, (2dc in next st) 3 times, 9dc, (sk1, 2dc) 5 times, 7dc, sl1, cut yarn and draw through loop on hook to finish.

v
Foundation row: Ch33, turn.
Round 1: Working in 2nd st from hook, 14dc, decrease 2 across next 3 sts (push hook through next st, sk1 st, push hook through next st, wrap yarn around hook and pull through all sts on hook), 14dc, 3dc in end st.
Round 2: Now work along other side of foundation chain 15dc, 3dc in end st, 15dc, 2dc in next st, 12dc, decrease 4 across next 5 sts (push hook through next st, sk3 sts, push hook through next st, wrap yarn around hook and pull through all sts on hook), 12dc, 3dc in next 3 sts.
Round 3: (15dc, 2dc in next 3 sts) twice, 10dc, decrease 4 across next 5 sts (push hook through next st, sk3 sts, push hook through next st, wrap yarn around hook and pull through all sts on hook), 10dc, sl1, cut yarn and draw through loop on hook to finish.

w
Foundation row: Ch40, turn.
Round 1: Working in 2nd st from hook, 15dc, ch24, turn, working in 2nd st from hook, 23dc, 23dc along original foundation chain, 3dc in end st.
Round 2: Now work along other side of foundation chain, 12dc, (sk1, 1dc) 7 times, 10dc, 3dc in end st, 12dc, (sk1, 1dc) 7 times, 12dc, 3dc in end st, 8dc, sk2, 7dc, (2dc in next st, 1dc) 3 times, (1dc, skip 1) twice, (1dc, 2dc in next st) 3 times, 15dc,

3dc in end st.
Round 3: 10dc, (sk1, 1dc) 5 times, 10dc, (2dc in next st) 3 times, 10dc, (sk1, 1dc) 5 times, 11dc, (2dc in next st) 3 times, 23dc, sk1, sl1, 24dc, sl1, cut yarn and draw through loop on hook to finish.

x

Foundation row: Ch25, turn.
Round 1: Working in 2nd st from hook, 10dc, sl1, ch12, working in 2nd st from hook, 11dc, sl1, ch12, working in 2nd st from hook, 11dc, sl1 in next st on original foundation row, ch12, 11dc, 3dc in end st.
Round 2: (8dc, sl1, sk4, sl1, 8dc, 3dc in end st) 4 times.
Round 3: (7dc, sl1, sk2, sl1, 7dc, 2dc in next 3 sts) 3 times, 7dc, sl1, sk2, sl1, 7dc, sl1, cut yarn and draw through loop on hook to finish.

y

Foundation row: Ch20, turn.
Round 1: Working in 2nd st from hook, 9dc, sl1, ch10, working in 2nd st from hook, 8dc, sl1 in st next to ch10, 9dc, 3dc in end st.
Round 2: 7dc, sk2, 7dc, 3dc in end st, 8dc, sl1, sk4, sl1, 4dc, (2dc in next st) 3 times.
Round 3: 9dc, sk1, 6dc, 2dc in next 3 sts, 6dc, sl1, 8dc, (2dc in next st) 3 times, 7dc, sl1, 7dc, (2dc in next st) 3 times, 16dc, sl1, cut yarn and draw through loop on hook to finish.

z

Foundation row: Ch40, turn, working in 2nd st from hook, 38dc, 3dc in last st, turn.
Round 1: 9dc, sl1, sk2, sl1, 14dc, 2dc in next 2 sts, 8dc, 3dc in end st.
Round 2: 8dc, sl1, sk2, sl1, 14dc, 2dc in next 2 sts, 10dc, 3dc in end st, 7dc, push hook through next st and following 5th st, wrap yarn and draw through all loops on hook to sl1, 11dc, 2dc in next 3 sts, 7dc, 2dc in next 3 sts, 5dc, push hook through next st and following 7th st, wrap yarn and draw through all loops on hook to sl1, 12dc, 2dc in next 3 sts, 11dc, sl1, cut yarn and draw through loop on hook to finish.

Heart

Using 4mm (US G/6) hook, ch4 and join with sl st to form a ring.
Round 1: Ch3 (counts as 1tr), 2tr in ring, [ch2, 3tr in ring] 3 times, ch2, join with sl st to 3rd ch.
Round 2: Ch3 (counts as 1tr), 1tr between first 2tr, 1tr between next 2tr, [2tr, ch2, 2tr] in corner space, *(1tr between next 2tr) twice, [2tr, ch2, 2tr] in corner space, rep from * once more, (1tr between next 2tr) twice, [2tr, ch2, 1tr] in corner space, sl st to 3rd ch. Fasten off.

Top right section of heart

Rejoin yarn between 3rd and 4th tr of one side and work as follows:
Next round: Ch3 (counts as 1tr), 5tr in same space at bottom of chain, 6dtr in same space. Fasten off.

Top left section of heart

Rejoin yarn between 3rd and 4th tr of next side and work as follows:
Next round: Ch4 (counts as 1dtr), 5dtr in same space at bottom of chain, 6tr in same space. Fasten off.

To finish

With RS facing and using contrast colour, rejoin yarn to ch2-sp at bottom of heart and work as follows:
Ch1, 2dc in same space, 1dc in each of next 6tr, 2dc in next ch2-sp, 1dc in each of next 6tr and 6dtr of right section of heart, 3dc in next ch2-sp, 1dc in each of next 6dtr and 6tr of left section of heart, 2dc in next ch2-sp, 1dc in next 6tr. Join with sl st to 1st ch.
Fasten off. Weave in any yarn ends.

INTERMEDIATE

Chevron Throw

A great way to show off your crafty side at home, this throw uses stylish colours in a random stripe repeat. Crocheted in super chunky 100% merino wool for luxurious cosiness, It's reversible, so there is no right or wrong side – just drape it across the sofa, over the end of the bed, on an armchair or around your shoulders.

Measurements
One size
Approx. 105cm (41½ in) wide x 145cm (57 in) long

What you will need
- Wool Couture Cheeky Chunky 100% merino wool, 65m (71 yards) per 100g (3½ oz)

Quantity:
- **A** 4 x 100g (3½ oz) balls in Black
- **B** 5 x 100g (3½ oz) balls in Cinnamon
- **C** 2 x 100g (3½ oz) balls in Aquamarine
- **D** 3 x 100g (3½ oz) balls in Gold
- **E** 2 x 100g (3½ oz) balls in Natural Cream
- 12mm (US P/16) crochet hook
- Yarn needle

Tension (gauge)
16 sts to 17cm (6¾ in) and 10 rows to 20cm (8 in) using 12mm (US P/16) hook, or size required to achieve the correct tension (gauge).

Abbreviations
See page 61.

Special techniques
Creating a ridge effect (see page 155).

Notes
Join in every new colour on the last stitch of the row and leave a long end when cutting the yarn to weave in when you have finished. To join colour, insert hook in last stitch, yarn around hook with current colour and pull loop through, drop current colour, pick up next colour, yarn around hook with next colour and pull through both loops to complete the dc. Next colour is now on the hook.

Crochet Homewares

To make

80-row stripe sequence

1 row A	1 row A
3 rows B	1 row E
1 row C	4 rows D
1 row A	1 row A
2 rows D	3 rows B
1 row E	1 row C
2 rows A	1 row A
1 row E	2 rows D
3 rows C	1 row E
4 rows B	2 rows A
1 row A	1 row E
2 rows E	3 rows C
1 row D	4 rows B
1 row A	1 row A
2 rows B	2 rows E
1 row C	1 row D
1 row A	1 row A
3 rows D	2 rows B
1 row E	1 row C
2 rows A	1 row A
1 row E	3 rows D
3 rows C	1 row E
2 rows B	2 rows A

Throw

Using 12mm (US P/16) hook and **A**, ch116 loosely and work as follows:

Row 1 (RS): Insert hook in 3rd ch from hook, yrh and draw through a loop, insert hook in next ch, yrh and draw through a loop, yrh and draw through all 3 loops on hook (counts as first dc3tog), **1dc into each of next 6 ch, 3dc into next ch, 1dc in each of next 6 ch, *insert hook in next ch, yrh and draw through a loop*, rep from * to * twice more, yrh and draw through all 4 loops on hook (called dc3tog), rep from ** to end. Change to **B** when finishing the last st of row (see Notes on page 153), turn.

Note: From this point, insert hook into back loop only of each st throughout and continue in colours as set by 80-row stripe sequence.

Row 2: Ch2, insert hook in st at base of ch2, yrh and draw through a loop, insert hook in next st, yrh and draw through a loop, yrh and draw through all 3 loops on hook (counts as first dc3tog), *1dc in each of next 6 sts, 3dc in next dc, 1dc in each of next 6 sts, dc3tog, rep from * ending last rep by working last step of dc3tog into 2nd of beg ch2 of previous row, turn.

Row 2 is repeated throughout following the stripe sequence. The first 2 rows of the stripe sequence have already been worked. Tick off the rows as you complete them.

To finish

Weave in any yarn ends.

Masterclass

Creating a ridge effect

Rather than inserting the hook through both strands at the top of a stitch in the row below to make a new stitch, working into the back strand only makes an attractive ridged line along the row at the front of the work. This is because the front strand that isn't worked is pushed onto the surface of the crochet and becomes a decorative detail. For this throw, the technique of working into the back loop only is used in combination with a series of increases and decreases to create the chevron design with added texture.

One Looking at the rope of chains that sit on the top of the row just completed, identify the back strand of the first chain. Whereas you would ordinarily work through both strands, here insert the hook through the back strand only.

Two Finish the stitch as usual. You will see how working through the back strand only as forced the front strand to sit on the surface of the work and has formed a ridge.

Crochet Homewares

Granny Square Cushion

EASY

The ubiquitous granny square is probably one of the best-known crochet patterns and one of the first things I learned how to crochet from a YouTube tutorial. Easy to grasp, this traditional motif takes on a contemporary feel when scaled up to cushion size. Make two, sew them together, and… "ta dah"… a cushion!

Measurements
One size
50cm (19¾ in) x 50cm (19¾ in)

What you will need
- Wool Couture Cheeky Chunky 100% merino wool, 65m (71 yards) per 100g (3½ oz)

Quantity:
- **A** 1 x 100g (3½ oz) ball in Gold
- **B** 1 x 100g (3½ oz) ball in Aquamarine
- **C** 1 x 100g (3½ oz) ball in Natural Cream
- **D** 1 x 100g (3½ oz) ball in Black

- 12mm (US P/16) hook
- 50cm (19¾ in) square cushion pad (pillow insert)
- Yarn needle

Tension (gauge)
7 tr to 10cm (4 in) and 4 rows to 11cm (4½ in) over patt using 12mm (US P/16) hook, or size required to achieve the correct tension (gauge).

Abbreviations
See page 61.

Special technique
Joining on a new colour (see page 159).

To make

Back and front (both alike)

Base ring: Using 12mm (US P/16) hook and **A**, ch4, join with a sl st in 1st ch to form a ring.
Round 1 (RS): Ch5 (counts as 1tr and 2ch), (3tr in ring, ch2) 3 times, 2tr in ring, join with a sl st to 3rd ch of beg ch5. *4 groups of 3tr and 4 ch2-sps.*
Fasten off.
Round 2: Using **B**, rejoin yarn with a sl st in any corner ch2-sp, ch7 (counts as 1tr and ch4), *2tr in same ch2-sp, 1tr in each tr across side of square to next corner ch2-sp**, 2tr in next ch2-sp, ch4, rep from * twice more and from * to ** again, 1tr in same sp as beg ch7, sl st to 3rd ch of beg ch7. *4 groups of 7tr and 4 ch4-sps.*
Fasten off.
Round 3: Using **C**, as Round 2. *4 groups of 11tr and 4 ch4-sps.*
Fasten off.
Round 4: Using **D**, as Round 2. *4 groups of 15tr and 4 ch4-sps.*
Fasten off.
Round 5: Using **B**, as Round 2. *4 groups of 19tr and 4 ch4-sps.*
Fasten off.
Round 6: Using **A**, as Round 2. *4 groups of 23tr and 4 ch4-sps.*
Fasten off.
Round 7: Using **C**, as Round 2. *4 groups of 27tr and 4 ch4-sps.*
Fasten off.
Round 8: Using **D**, Using D, as Round 2. *4 groups of 31tr and 4 ch4-sps.*
Fasten off.

To finish

Weave in any yarn ends. You may wish to cover your cushion pad (pillow insert) in black fabric, or a contrast colour to show through the spaces in the crochet.
Join three sides of cushion cover using whip stitch. Insert the cushion pad (pillow insert) and close the final seam.

Masterclass

Joining on a new colour

When bringing in a new colour at the beginning of a motif round, fasten off the old colour and join on a new colour with a slip stitch. Joining on the new colour with a slip stitch makes a firm attachment.

One   Make a slip knot with the new colour. Insert the hook at the position on the motif instructed by the pattern and draw the slip knot through.

Two   Start the new round with the specified numbers of chains, drawing the first chain through the slip knot.

Three   Work the stitches of the round over both yarn tails (the new colour and the old colour), so there are fewer ends to darn in later. Alternatively, to reduce bulk, start the new colour in a different place and weave in one tail at a time.

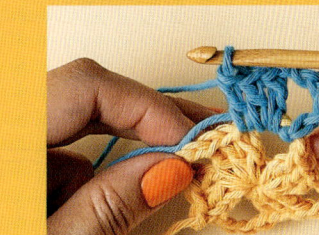

Four   When you reach each corner of the previous round, after working the specified number of stitches, remember to work a number of chains to form the corners of the current round.

Five   When the motif is finished, trim the yarn ends that have been worked over back to neaten, but do not snip them too close to the stitches as that way they would be more likely to unravel.

Crochet Homewares

EMBRACE YOUR

CREATIVITY

Caring For Your Makes

Aftercare

When you've invested so much time in creating a handmade piece, it's really important to care for your crocheted projects. If properly looked after, they can last for many years to come – for example, items that you've made for your kids could be passed onto their children. Here are some of the best ways to care for your crochet once made and worn.

• Laundering

The most important thing when laundering an item is to follow the care instructions on the yarn label or ball band for washing or dry cleaning. I keep the yarn label in a folder or take a photo and store it on my phone. On the rare occasion a yarn label says dry clean only, remember to take the label with you to the dry cleaners, so they use the correct solvents. If something is labelled as dry clean only, you may be able to hand wash it in cold water, but always check first using a crocheted tension (gauge) swatch to see what happens!

Some yarns, like acrylic or cotton, can go into the washing machine on a cold, gentle wash cycle but most animal fibres need to be hand-washed. Never wash a wool item in hot water because this will make it become "felted", where the fabric becomes tighter and stiffer, rather than softer or more fluid. Unless this is the effect you are going for, in which case, wash away!

If your item is made up of more than one yarn, always use the gentlest method of washing. So, if you have two yarns and one says dry clean only and the other allows for machine washing, stick to dry cleaning.

Whether hand washing or machine washing, always use a specially formulated wash for wool and other animal fibres or a mild detergent, which is designed for delicate fabrics. Always follow the instructions when it comes to how much wool wash or detergent to add. If something is going in the washing machine, place the detergent in the dispenser drawer rather than directly in the drum, so it does not create any unnecessary friction during the wash cycle that could damage your item.

When you are hand washing an item, use a decent-sized bowl or sink where there is space to submerge your item and for water to flow around it easily. Fill the bowl or sink with water, add the wool wash and mix this in properly before adding your item. Be gentle with it – so give it a good dunk and swish the water around it rather than kneading or scrubbing. If the water goes dirty quite quickly, don't be surprised. Hand-wash items are laundered less frequently than machine-wash ones, so they will gather dirt and oils that will swiftly leech into the water. If the water becomes murky, you can always drain it away, squeezing your item as you do so. Do not lift the item out of the sink or bowl because the weight of the water can pull it out of shape.

Nowadays, most commercially available yarns are colorfast, but it is always worth doublechecking. Take a length of yarn, wet it thoroughly and then wrap it tightly around a sheet of white paper towel. Leave the yarn to dry, then unwind it from the paper towel. If it has left behind any mark then the yarn is not colorfast.

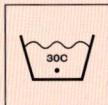
Machine wash on cold cycle

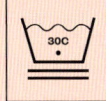
Machine wash on gentle cycle

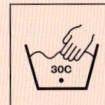
Hand wash in cold water

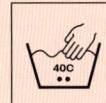
Hand wash in warm water

Do not bleach

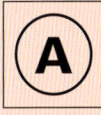
Dry-cleanable in any solvent

Dry-cleanable in certain solvent

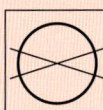
Do not dry clean

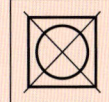
Do not tumble dry

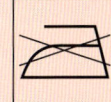
Do not iron

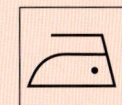
Iron on a low heat

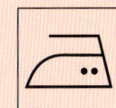
Iron on a medium heat

Caring For Your Makes

- **Removing stains**

We all have occasional accidents. In our house, spilling drinks is more of a regular occurrence. If your crochet has become stained for any reason, act swiftly. Immediately blot away any excess liquid or scrape off any solid matter. Next, put some mild detergent on a clean dishcloth and directly blot the stain. Be sure to dab the fabric rather than rub it, as this can damage the fibres. Soak washable garments in cold water for 30 minutes and then rinse as if you were washing and drying normally. Stubborn stains might need to be soaked longer, like overnight.

Different stains may require different treatments – some people swear by distilled white vinegar for getting rid of alcohol and coffee stains, whilst white spirit can work wonders on oily stains.

Always be sure to check that this will not damage the yarn and can be done safely. If your garment is too delicate (or the stain is too stubborn), your local dry cleaners will be able to advise you on the best way to get the stain out or even complete the stain removal for you.

- **Rinsing and drying**

After hand washing any items, rinse them thoroughly in cold water until the water runs clear – all the soap particles that may matt the fabric fibres or irritate sensitive skin need to be washed away. (Some specialist wool washes do not need rinsing out, so check the instructions on the bottle.) Do not wring out or twist the item to get rid of the water, instead gently squeeze out as much moisture as you can. Lift the item from the sink or basin, supporting it from underneath so that it doesn't sag, and then transfer to a clean, dry towel. Roll it up in the towel to press out even more water.

Lay the item flat on a second clean, dry towel to soak up any further moisture. Reshape the item by gently patting it out before leaving it somewhere to dry. Do not use coat hangers for drying garments because your items might stretch out of shape. You need to dry your item where the air can flow around it easily but away from a direct source of heat like a radiator and out of direct sunlight, so avoid resting items next to windows. Instead, lie flat and ease any garments into their original shape, carefully adjusting any ribbed bands at the waist, cuffs and neckline. Fold down any collars and fasten any buttons. Lay the arms flat. You may need to dry one side and then flip the item over to dry the other.

> (TOM'S TIP:)
>
> When you think about washing your sweater, ask yourself whether it could be aired instead. One of the best things about wool is that it stays fresher between washes than garments made of synthetics or cotton. Wool garments don't actually need laundering that frequently if they're well aired and rested between wears, so give them an air instead and use a liberal spritz of clothing mist spray to get rid of any odours and make them smell nice if you want. I read somewhere that "airing is caring", so follow this motto!

When drying larger items like blankets, re-position them frequently so they don't pull out of shape due to the weight of the water. Allow all items to dry for at least 24 hours, while larger items will need to be dried for at least 24 hours on each side.

If any yarn ends work themselves loose during laundering, don't be tempted to simply trim them away as this may lead to your work eventually unravelling. Pull any yarn ends all the way out and then sew them in properly again (see pages 71).

- **Ironing**

If your item is full of creases and needs to be ironed, proceed with caution! Always check the yarn label first and use the iron on a low setting. If the iron is too hot, this can cause discolouration and, in the worst cases, scorch marks on the fabric. Avoid this by pressing down very gently on a low heat, bearing in mind that most fibres need only a little steam to make the creases fall out.

- **Pilling**

There's nothing more annoying than those little bobbles of fluff that can appear on crocheted items over time. It happens when bits of fibre separate from the strand of yarn and then become agitated, so they roll up into little balls. Pilling tends to occur in areas where there's a lot of friction, such as the sides of a sweater or around the underarms. Resist the temptation to tug at them because this can pull more of the yarn away from the strand. Instead, comb or brush them away or, after going over the item with sticky tape, use a special shaving tool to gently remove them.

TOM'S TIP:

`Little hole in your sweater? Don't ignore it! Always repair any holes before laundering your item because the friction caused by washing can make any hole bigger. There are different ways to mend a hole, and one of these is visible mending (see page 179).`

- **Storing and protecting**

Once your items are clean and dry, store them carefully. If you're putting heavy wool sweaters away for the summer, the best options are polythene ziplock bags or airtight tubs. As well as keeping moths out, they minimise moisture and reduce the risk of mould. Some people also pop in a cedar ball or some dried lavender and sage to repel moths.

Moths love all natural fibres, including wool, cashmere, silk, and cotton because they contain a protein called keratin, which the larvae uses as nutrition. They have also been known to munch on acrylics, even though they hold no nutritional value.

It's really important to launder your items before you store them away. This will get rid of any larvae eggs and stains that could set in over time. It will also banish perspiration stains and other natural oils that are like candy to moths!

- **Folding**

Do you know how to properly fold a sweater? Never hang up your knitwear because it will stretch out of shape. Instead, fold a sweater or cardigan neatly to save space and avoid it having a hard crease down the front.

One: Lay your garment on a flat surface, front side facing down. Fold one side into the centre, then one sleeve down at an angle.

Two: Fold the second side into the centre and take the sleeve down at the same angle. Try to avoid the two sleeves overlapping.

Three: Lift the hem of the garment and fold the bottom third of the folded garment up to cover most of the sleeves.

Four: Lift the shoulders of the garment and fold the top third over the rest of the garment to make a neat package. Job done!

How to...

I love being part of a community of like-minded crafters, where everyone is really supportive and encouraging. Being able to use my social platforms to share ideas and get feedback from followers is amazing. Here are some of the best tips I've picked up that I hope will inspire you in the same way!

Gift your makes

I love giving hand-crocheted gifts and always include the yarn label or ball band so the recipient knows how to care for it. This is important for the longevity of the make, as some yarns need to be hand-washed (see pages 165–167).

One of the first things I did when I started crocheting was to order a batch of woven labels, just like the ones I had sewn into my school uniform. They say 'Made with Love by Tom Daley' in rainbow colours. I sent off for a load and so I always add them to items I've made. But I hate sewing them in, so I sometimes get my mum to do it for me!

If I'm giving an item as a gift, I fold it, wrap it in tissue paper and put it into a suitably sized box. Get creative with the wrapping, maybe by matching the gift wrap to your make. I like to use leftover yarn from the gift instead of a ribbon. You could even make a heart motif, a tassel or an initial letter (see pages 144–151) to decorate the parcel.

Once I've worn a garment a number of times, but then need to make space for some new makes, I often give it away to someone who I think will love it. If I've loved making it and wearing it, I figure that someone else will too! Why not customise it with embroidery or appliqué or encourage the recipient to do the same.

The longer we can keep existing clothes in our wardrobes and out of landfill the better it is for the planet. Handmade sweaters, blankets and other items can become treasured heirlooms for the next generation, made even more precious knowing that every stitch has been made with love.

Fit crochet into your day

Life can be busy but one of the great things about crochet is how portable it is. Here are my tips to make sure crafting is an everyday activity.

Take a portable project with you
If you're working on several projects, keep larger ones at home and choose a smaller and more portable one that you can take with you on the train during your commute, to the office for a few minutes crafting on your lunch break, or even at the side of the pool during a major sporting competition! I find that crochet is especially portable, particularly quick makes like the Friendship Bracelets (see pages 84–87) or motifs like the Heart Keyring (see pages 108–111).

Craft as you travel
Crochet is such a great way to occupy your mind (and hands) when travelling, which inevitably involves lots of waiting around at airports and stations. Whenever I travel with my synchronised diving partner Matty (Lee), he constantly complains that I'm elbowing him in the ribs because I'm concentrating on my crochet.

Crochet projects are brilliantly portable, just make sure you have the right kit and be realistic about what you can complete in the time you have. It's best to leave the complex patterns and colourwork at home. Always check with your airline first, but generally you're allowed to carry both crochet hooks and knitting needles in cabin and hold luggage. However, only small scissors are allowed in cabin luggage, so choose a neat pair of embroidery scissors for your travel craft kit.

Make it a priority
If you find yourself spending hours watching TV or scrolling through social media feeds most evenings, why not focus on your crochet instead? Make it a priority and part of your everyday routine and your skills will soon come on in leaps and bounds. It's a great way to keep your hands busy rather than doom-scrolling on your phone!

Use it as an incentive
If I've got work or chores to do that I've been putting off, I tell myself that once they're completed, then I can reward myself with a few hours crocheting or planning a new project. Invariably I get whatever I need to do completed much quicker this way. I also use it as a re-set to refresh my mind when going between different parts of my day – like from a meeting with my agent to picking my son up from school. It's a great way to leave work behind and get back to me.

Join a group
I've found the crafting community to be such an amazing place to hang out. Everyone has something in common, wherever you are from no matter what your age. I think these groups are a great way to dedicate time to crochet and make some new friends as well. If you can't find a group local to you, why not set one up at home, in your favourite pub or café, or local community space.

Complete every project
Loads of crafters abandon a project halfway through, leading to a high number of UFOs (un-finished objects). This can be demoralising, so I don't distract myself with new yarns or design ideas before I completing the one I'm currently working on. Sometimes it's the very last stage of a make, the sewing up, that prevents you from completing a project. If this is the case, why not plump for those projects that are crocheted in the round for a seam-free, no-sewing-up-required make. I love the satisfaction of finishing something I've been working on. It's so rewarding when you can try it on, or gift it to a friend.

Manage your yarn stash

Wondering how you can take control of your growing yarn stash? If you're into crafting the chances are you will accumulate lots of yarn. I often buy a bit too much yarn for a project, so I try to create something from my surplus. Several projects in this book make great stash-busters, including the Friendship Bracelets (see pages 84–87), the Heart Keyring (see pages 108–111), the Random Stripe Sweater (see pages 128–132) and the Plant Pots (see pages 136–139). There are loads of different ways you can manage your yarn stash, but here are my tips.

Keep it all in one place

This might sound obvious, but it makes sense to have all your yarn stored in one location. You will also need to decide how to keep it – whether that's in clear plastic or wire boxes or somewhere else, like a re-purposed cabinet or bookshelf, or even a spare wall. If, like me, you're running out of room, always make use of vertical wall space. I keep mine in my closet where I have a special circular storage area. Then I have some overflow in extra wire baskets.

Have somewhere for your WIP

If you have a WIP (work in progress), keep all the yarn and bits 'n' bobs for that project together in one place. I keep mine in my Team Great Knittin' tote bag, so I can carry it around with me when I'm on the go.

Decide how to organise it

Group your yarns in whatever way makes the most sense to you: that could be by colour, weight, fibre or brand. If you divide your yarn into boxes in a particular way, they can be labelled, so you can find any yarn more easily. Originally, I sorted my yarns by colour. While I liked the fact that I could respond to the colours when starting a new project, I found that wasn't the best way for me. Now it's more random, but that works. It's creative chaos, which leads to some unexpected results. Don't be disheartened if you see Instagram posts of other people's incredible, well-organised yarn stashes; they never stay that way for long. It's always better to use up yarn than to hoard it.

Make balls from loose yarn

If you have lots of loose bits of yarn, these can really easily become tangled, so I've found one of the best ways to stay organised is by making sure all my yarn is in some kind of structure. I like to wind my yarn into balls. Always keep the yarn label (ball band) so you know what the weight, fibre and care instructions are – the easiest way to do this is to tuck the label into the ball. This is a great opportunity to take an inventory of what you have, so you can start planning what you can make with this yarn – like a Random Stripe Sweater (see pages 128–132) or pompoms for your Cosy Slippers (see pages 102–107). If you don't think you will use a yarn, gift it to another crafter or donate it to a charity shop, retirement home or college, so someone else can make good use of it. You can also keep all your little bits of yarn that are too small for anything else together in a jar to use as stuffing for toys. Put any other crafty off-cuts, like felt or material, in there too.

Organise your other supplies

As well as organising your yarn, take the opportunity to sort out your other crafting supplies at the same time. Group crochet hooks together using hairbands and make sure everything is labelled. Some people keep crochet hooks in pencil cases, bottles, or jars. I keep mine in a drawer with a cutlery tray insert.

TOM'S TIP:

```
I always advise keeping yarn off the
floor, away from dust, pets and any
creepy-crawlies. Water is also a no-no.
A great way to store yarn is in vacuum-
packed bags because these will also
keep out moths, who just love to munch
through those delicious natural fibres.
```

Caring For Your Makes

Be mindful while you make

Crochet is an amazing tool for mindfulness and relaxation. For me, it's an important form of self-care and helps me to remain calm, even in stressful situations. Clinically proven to reduce anxiety, relieve stress, and re-focus the mind, crochet is thought to improve self-esteem because you're left with something tangible at the end. Practice stimulates the whole brain and is even believed to slow cognitive decline.

Focus on your breath

All mindfulness and meditation practice focuses on the breath. Think about slowing your inhalations, taking a few seconds longer to exhale, if possible. This will engage your parasympathetic nervous system and turn the dial down on your sympathetic nervous system. This means your heart rate will drop, your blood pressure will lower, and you will be in a state of calm as you crochet.

Challenge yourself

Practising crochet allows you focus on what you're doing and the stitches in hand. Try to not let your mind wander to thoughts of the past, future, or your to-do list. If you find your mind drifting on to what you're going to cook for dinner, or whether you've remembered to feed the cat, it might be a good opportunity to try a more complex stitch which requires your full attention. I find that even the simple task of counting stitches is a great way to remain in the moment with my crochet.

Create a space to craft

If you're trying to craft more mindfully, find a quiet space to work away from too many distractions (turn off the TV and put your phone on silent). Find a comfortable spot and give yourself time to sit and relax. When I'm not crocheting poolside, I love to craft outside because I find being in nature very calming. At home I like to sit at the kitchen table. Personally, I find the table better for my posture as it supports my elbows. Sometimes I'll light a scented candle or play music while I work.

Engage your senses

Crochet is a wonderfully sensory activity. Consider the tactile qualities of the yarn as it moves through your fingers. Enjoy the weight of the work in your lap. Employ all your senses.

Reflect on your crafting

Take time to think about your crochet journey, including how it fits into your life, how your projects have worked out, how the physical aspects of crochet feel, perhaps even how it's changed your life.

"Crochet *keeps* me *from* unravelling."

TOM DALEY

"

Crochet with upcycled yarns

I'm trying to make more sustainable and eco-friendly choices. Making clothes slowly by hand is already a more planet-friendly choice than buying ready-to-wear fast fashion. But I'm also learning more about the yarns that I choose to craft with. You can buy yarns made from recycled fibres or even create your own upcycled yarn out of textiles that you already have at home. Why not cut up worn-out t-shirts into continuous strips to crochet with (see page 127) or unravel a tired old sweater and re-use the yarn to make something new. (This is known as "frogging" because when you "rip it" back, it sounds like "ribbit, ribbit" – the noise a frog makes!)

There are loads of added advantages to crocheting with recycled yarns. Not only does it do less harm to the planet, by reducing and reusing waste that may end up going to landfill sites, but it can save you money too. It can also be a great way of finding unusual and unique yarns to work with. Win, win.

What are recycled yarns?
Recycled yarns are either made from pre- or post-consumer recycled fibres, such as plastic bottles or denim jeans or recycled textiles. The fibres are broken down, re-spun and blended with other fibres such as cotton to create new yarns.

Where can you buy them?
If you choose to purchase recycled yarns, there are many choices from big brand names to smaller indie spinners. Check out your local yarn store or favourite online retailer and ask them for recommendations for eco-friendly yarns. You can also scour charity shops, thrift stores and yard sales for hand-knitted or crocheted garments to upcycle. Just remember to check how they are constructed to ensure they can be frogged (unravelled) and that you can reclaim the yarn.

How do I unravel an old garment?
Start by finding the edges and unpicking the seams carefully by cutting through the sewing stitches. Don't make the mistake of chopping the wrong bit! Simply start from the cast-off edge and unravel the yarn with care, rolling the yarn into a ball as you go. This ball will grow as the garment shrinks!

What do I need to know?
Crocheting with recycled yarns is a slightly different experience from working with new yarns. Check the garment for any labels containing care instructions before frogging, and you may wish to hand wash the item in a delicate detergent and leave to dry flat before you begin to unravel it. Sometimes the old yarn can retain the shape of its previous life and not be as smooth. All natural fibres such as 100% wool will be better for re-use, but you may need to steam the yarn before you work with it to help the fibres relax.

What about colour?
Be aware that colours may not be consistent and may vary from one ball to another. Weigh the yarn to ensure you have enough for your project, or incorporate the variations into your design by using stripes or colour blocking. Yarns can also be re-dyed (or over-dyed), but always check the fibre content and test a small swatch first.

Prolong the life of a garment

When unpacking last winter's knits, or rediscovering an old-friend sweater at the back of your wardrobe, you might find a few unexpected holes that weren't there before. Wear and tear over time, particularly on the heels of socks or the elbows of sweaters, as well as moths who love to eat natural fibres, will inevitably result in a few holes (see page 168). But rather than consigning a treasured make to the trash or recycling, see this as another opportunity to customise a garment and make it your own.

Darning
The traditional technique of darning has long been used to make small repairs when holes appear in an item. It's a thrifty way to extend the life of a garment. Essentially, you stitch a square of simple running stitches around the hole, leaving a good margin all the way round, then you weave the yarn back and forth between the running stitches to patch over the hole.

You can use the same yarn and colour to darn over a hole so that it's practically invisible, however I love using a technique called visible mending to make a deliberate feature of the repair. Practitioners like Celia Pym and Tomofholland have made visible mending on both knitting and crochet into an art form.

Appliqué
Instead of using contrasting colour threads to visibly darn over an area, you could cover it completely with a patch, such as a crocheted motif or letter – just appliqué the new patch over the existing hole. It's a really fun and creative way to extend the life of your garment and give your much-loved piece an even more individual edge.

There are loads of other techniques you might like to try, such as embroidery, darning, appliqué, and sashiko. YouTube is your friend when it comes to looking up ideas and experimenting.

Own your making

When it comes to developing your own style of crochet, there are no rights or wrongs. Whether you want to try something new, completely overhaul your wardrobe or become the next street-style sensation – anything goes!

Find the silhouettes you love

Part of feeling confident in your handmade garments is finding shapes and textures that make you feel good. Start by looking at the most-worn pieces already in your wardrobe. Think about why those items are your faves and note down the design elements that you love – it could be a roll-neck sweater, a cropped sleeveless vest or a shawl-collar cardigan that are all great for layering. I love oversized sweaters, and find that using a chunky yarn creates really cosy garments.

Recreate the catwalk

I love seeing the latest designs from fashion houses on the catwalk. One of the best things about being able to crochet and knit is that you can recreate designer styles for a fraction of the price. My interpretation of a monochrome Gucci dress that I crocheted for my friend Sophie was really fun to make and cost me £10 in yarn! I also knitted my version of JW Anderson's patchwork cardigan, made famous by Harry Styles – it cost me less than a tenth of the original price.

Create a mood board

To figure out your style, create a mood board of outfits you love. Online, you can pin images to boards on Pinterest or bookmark photos into your saved folder on Instagram. Offline, you can go old-school by tearing out pages from magazines and pasting them onto card or fixing them to a pinboard. Your mood board doesn't have to feature crocheted garments. Anything can be inspiration…

Break the rules

Making something unique means you're no longer restricted to what you can find on the high street. It can be a bit nerve-wracking trying new looks and stepping out of your comfort zone, but your confidence will grow the more you do it. Experiment with external seams, visible yarn ends or embroidered motifs in your work. If you fancy embroidering your pet cat onto your sweater, do it!

Look to other knitters

I find that talking about crochet and crafting with like-minded makers can inspire me and provide style ideas. I love browsing patterns online and in magazines. It can be inspiring to look at the work of extreme crafters – a group of exuberant yarn designers re-imagining the entire craft.

"Every *piece* is unique to *you.*"

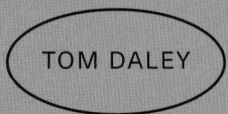
TOM DALEY

Recommended Yarns

There is a yarn specified for each of the project designs in this book. You can stick with the recommended yarn. If so, you just need to pick your favourite shade. However, if you want to use a different yarn to the one specified in the pattern, you need to compare the tension (gauge) given on the yarn label (ball band) to be confident that the finished result and dimensions will not differ too dramatically from the project measurements given. The yarns used throughout this book are listed below in alphabetical order.

Erika Knight Studio Linen
85% recycled linen, 15% linen
120m (131 yards) per 50g (1¾ oz)
21 sts to 10cm (4 in) on
3.5–4mm (US 4–6)
www.erikaknight.co.uk

Kremke Soul Wool Karma Cotton
70% cotton, 30% recycled polyamide
105m (115 yards) per 50g (1¾ oz)
18 sts x 26 rows to 10cm (4 in) on 3–4mm (US 3–6)
www.kremkegarne.de

Kremke Soul Wool Morning Salutation Vegan
51% lyocell, 49% cotton
110m (120 yards) per 50g (1¾ oz)
20 sts to 10cm (4 in) on 3–4mm (US 3–0)
www.kremkegarne.de

Wool Couture Cheeky Chunky
100% merino wool
65m (71 yards) per 100g (3½ oz)
10 sts x 12 rows to 10cm (4 in) on 10mm (US 15)
www.woolcouturecompany.com

Paintbox Yarns Cotton Aran
100% cotton
85m (93 yards) per 50g (1¾ oz)
20 sts x 24 rows to 10cm (4 in) on 4.5mm (US 7)
www.lovecrafts.com

Rico Essentials Cotton DK
100% cotton
120m (131 yards) per 50g (1¾ oz)
22 sts x 28 rows to 10cm (4 in) on 3–4mm (US 3–6)
www.rico-design.com

Wool and the Gang RaRa Raffia
100% paper
250m (273 yards) per 100g (3½ oz)
19 sts x 16 rows (single crochet) on 4.5mm (US 7)
www.woolandthegang.com

And for buttons
Textile Garden
www.textilegarden.com

Thank you ☺

I feel so lucky to be able to write a book about something that I love so much. When I first picked up a crochet hook and some yarn, I could not have imagined that crocheting would soon turn into one of my greatest passions.

A huge thank you to:

The team at YMU – Alex McGuire, Holly Bott, Amanda Harris, and Elise Middleton, for your continued support and help.

To the HQ team and everyone involved in creating my book, including Erika Knight and Arabella Harris at KnightKraft, Louise McKeever, Lisa Pendreigh, and Georgina Rodgers, and to the hugely talented creative team I worked with on the photoshoots, including Nikki Dupin and Emma Wells at Studio Nic&Lou. This process has been so enjoyable – thanks so much for making it a lot of fun! I am so grateful for everyone's hard work and energy in helping me realise my vision.

To Lance for introducing me to crafting (and never moaning about my growing yarn stash!) and to Robbie and Phoenix, my family and friends for appreciating my handmade gifts and cheering on my making.

To my fellow crocheters – and Team Great Knittin' – I can't wait to see what we make next!

#MadeWithLoveGetYourKnitsOut

An imprint of HarperCollins*Publishers* Ltd
1 London Bridge Street, London, SE1 9GF

www.harpercollins.co.uk

HarperCollins*Publishers*
Macken House, 39/40 Mayor Street Upper,
Dublin 1, D01 C9W8, Ireland

10 9 8 7 6 5 4 3 2 1

First published in Great Britain by
HQ, an imprint of HarperCollinsPublishers Ltd 2025

Copyright © Tom Daley 2024
Including patterns that first appeared in Made With Love 2024

Tom Daley asserts the moral right to be identified as the author of this work.
A catalogue record for this book is available from the British Library.

ISBN 978-0-00-865701-7

This book contains FSC™ certified paper and other controlled
sources to ensure responsible forest management.

For more information visit:
www.harpercollins.co.uk/green

Printed and bound in Malaysia by Papercraft

Editorial Director: Louise McKeever
Project Editor: Lisa Pendreigh
Project Design Consultants: Erika Knight and Arabella Harris at KnightKraft
Pattern Grading: Rosee Woodland for Light Work Collective
Pattern Technical Editing and Proofing: Helen Birch, Tricia Gilbert, Amelia Hodsdon,
Faye Perriam-Reed and Lynne Rowe for Light Work Collective
Knitters and Crocheters: Judith Cheek, Gillian Ely, Sarah Ford, Lucinda Ganderton, Erika Knight,
Sally Lee, Joanne Marsh, Lisa Pendreigh, Karin Rayner, Jemima Schlee and Juliana Yeo
Photography: Daniel Fraser
Photography Assistant: Andreas Parperi
Art Direction and Design: Nikki Dupin and Emma Wells @ Studio Nic&Lou
Models: Minmie @ iMM, Naomy @ Body London and Alanna @ Bruce and Brown
Casting production: Bella Robinson
Styling: Sairey Stemp
Hair and Makeup: Liz Martins and Brady Lea
Step photography: Cara Cormack
Hand model: Chinh Hoang
Senior Production Controller: Halema Begum

All rights reserved. No part of this publication may be reproduced, stored in a retrieval system,
or transmitted, in any form or by any means, electronic, mechanical, photocopying, recording or
otherwise, without the prior permission of the publishers.

This book is sold subject to the condition that it shall not, by way of trade or otherwise,
be lent, re-sold, hired out or otherwise circulated without the publisher's prior consent in
any form of binding or cover other than that in which it is published and without a similar
condition including this condition being imposed on the subsequent purchaser.